A LITTLE PRINCESS

Gender and Empire

I0809301

TWAYNE'S MASTERWORK STUDIES

Robert Lecker, General Editor

A LITTLE PRINCESS

Gender and Empire

Roderick McGillis

TWAYNE PUBLISHERS
An Imprint of Simon & Schuster Macmillan
New York

PRENTICE HALL INTERNATIONAL
London Mexico City New Delhi Singapore Sydney Toronto

Twayne's Masterwork Studies No. 159

A Little Princess: Gender and Empire
Roderick McGillis

Copyright © 1996 by Twayne Publishers
All rights reserved. No part of this book may be reproduced or transmitted in any form or by any means, electronic or mechanical, including photocopying, recording, or by any information storage and retrieval system, without permission in writing from the Publisher.

Twayne Publishers
An Imprint of Simon & Schuster Macmillan
1633 Broadway
New York, New York 10019

Library of Congress Cataloging-in-Publication Data

McGillis, Roderick.
A little princess : gender and empire / by Roderick McGillis.
p. cm.—(Masterworks studies ; no. 159)
Includes bibliographical references and index.
ISBN 0-8057-8818-2 (cloth).— ISBN 0-8057-8819-0 (pbk.)
1. Children's stories, American—History and criticism. 2. Children's stories, English—History and criticism. 3. Imperialism in literature. 4. Feminism and literature. 5. Sex role in literature. 6. Orphans in literature. 7. Girls in literature. [1. Burnett, Frances Hodgson, 1849–1924. Little princess.] I. Title. II. Series : Twayne's masterwork studies ; no. 159.
PS1214.L53M37 1996
813'.4—dc20 95-52736
CIP

The paper used in this publication meets the minimum requirements of American National Standard for Information Sciences—Permanence of Paper for Printed Library Materials. ANSI Z39.48-1984. ∞™

10 9 8 7 6 5 4 3 2 1 (hc)
10 9 8 7 6 5 4 3 2 1 (pb)

Printed in the United States of America

Contents

"SHE SLOWLY ADVANCED INTO THE PARLOR, CLUTCHING HER DOLL."

Sara Crewe and Miss Minchin.

Illustration by Reginald Birch from Sara Crewe; or, What Happened at Miss Minchin's, *by Frances Hodgson Burnett (New York: Charles Scribner's Sons, 1892), 15.*

Note on the References and Acknowledgments

Two years ago Robert Lecker invited me to participate in Twayne's Masterwork Studies series, and I acknowledge his confidence in me. Had I received a choice, I suspect that *A Little Princess* would not have been the book selected. Of nineteenth-century writers for children, several I enjoy as much as or more than I do Burnett, and in Burnett's canon I would have chosen *The Secret Garden* as the focus of my work. *A Little Princess* has raised more issues than I imagined it would, however, and I am pleased to have had the opportunity to work on it. For this opportunity I have to thank not only Robert Lecker but also Sylvia Miller, my editor at Twayne, for her patience, understanding, and acumen.

Work on this volume coincided with my supervision of Mavis Reimer's doctoral thesis on L.T. Meade, a contemporary of Burnett's, and I have benefited from Mavis's work. Everyone working on Burnett is indebted to Anne Thwaite's biography. Other work that has proved valuable to me is that of Phyllis Bixler, Elizabeth Keyser, and Susan Naramore Maher, whose paper on *A Little Princess* delivered at the 1993 Children's Literature Association Conference in Fredericton, New Brunswick, prompted my thinking at the outset of this project. I must also thank the Inter-Library Loans staff at the McKimmie Library, University of Calgary, for their help in getting me a copy of the play version of *A Little Princess*. Most useful and pleasant of all was my week at the Osborne Collection, Boys and Girls House, Toronto Public Library. Margaret Crawford Maloney and her staff were prompt and obliging, as well as friendly and warm. The Boys and Girls House, with its Osborne and Lillian H. Smith Collections, is truly a delightful and thorough research library.

I have consulted first editions of both *Sara Crewe* and *A Little Princess,* as my Bibliography indicates. Citations from *A Little Princess,* however, are from the Puffin edition that first appeared in 1961 and is still readily available. My range of reference is fairly small, but no one working in late nineteenth-century children's books can fail to have found useful Claudia Nelson's *Boys Will Be Girls* (1991) and Kimberly Reynolds's *Girls Only?* (1990), neither of which shows up in my Bibliography. I have also added a section to the Bibliography containing primary texts other than Burnett's to which I refer. Often these books do not come in for analysis in my text; I list them to offer the reader a beginning for contextualizing Burnett's work.

Finally, I must acknowledge once again the support of my family; Kate and Kyla are, as always, an inspiration. And Donna Batycki makes it all worthwhile.

Chronology: Frances Hodgson Burnett's Life and Works

1849	Frances Hodgson born 24 November in Manchester, England.
1853	Father, Edwin Hodgson, dies.
1855	Family moves to 16 Islington Square, Salford, in industrial surroundings.
1865	Family sails for North America and settles in New Market, Tennessee.
1866	Family moves near Knoxville, Tennessee, to a house called Noah's Ark; Frances spends much time outdoors, where she constructs a garden called "the Bower."
1868	"Hearts and Diamonds," Frances's first story, is published in *Godey's Lady's Book;* family lives in a house called Vagabondia.
1870	Mother, Eliza Hodgson (neé Boond), dies on 17 March; Frances is left in charge of family.
1873	Marries Dr. Swan Burnett on 19 September in New Market.
1874	Son Lionel born 20 September in Knoxville.
1875	Travels to Paris.
1876	Son Vivian born 5 April in Paris; returns to United States.
1877	Moves to Washington; publication of *That Lass o' Lowrie's.*
1879	Publication of *Haworth's;* first story appears in *St. Nicholas Magazine,* "Behind the White Brick."
1886	Publication of *Little Lord Fauntleroy.*
1887	Serial publication in *St. Nicholas Magazine* of *Sara Crewe; or, What Happened at Miss Minchin's* begins in December (concludes in February 1888).

1890	Begins relationship with Stephen Townsend; son Lionel dies.
1893	Publication of *The One I Knew the Best of All.*
1898	Divorces Swan Burnett; moves to Maytham Hall, Kent.
1900	Marries Stephen Townsend in Genoa, Italy, in February.
1902	The play *The Little Princess* opens at the Avenue Theatre in London; Burnett separates from Townsend.
1903	*The Little Princess* opens at the Criterion Theater in New York.
1905	Publication of *A Little Princess: Being the Whole Story of Sara Crewe Now Told for the First Time;* Burnett becomes U.S. citizen.
1906	Publication of *Racketty-Packetty House.*
1909	Moves to new home, Plandome, on Long Island.
1911	Publication of *The Secret Garden;* Burnett moves to Bermuda, where she lives on and off until 1920.
1915	Publication of *The Lost Prince.*
1924	Dies at Plandome, Long Island, on 29 October.

LITERARY AND HISTORICAL CONTEXT

1

Fairy Tale and Empire

In an undated letter to her longtime friend Richard Watson Gilder, an editor at Scribners, Frances Hodgson Burnett remarks that she is "re-working and developing for the Scribners the story of 'Sara Crewe.'" The story will now be, she says, "the nice, detaily kind of thing children love. You know, if anyone has muffins for tea, it delights children to know *why* they had muffins, and how the muffins were baked."[1] She finished the "re-working," and the Christmas book lists for 1905 contained (Warne in England, Scribners in America) a work whose full title is *A Little Princess: Being the Whole Story of Sara Crewe Now Told for the First Time.* As this title indicates, Burnett had told at least part of Sara Crewe's story before—twice before in fact. Her son Vivian informs us that she first began writing the story in 1885, but it didn't appear in the famous magazine for children, *St. Nicholas,* until December 1887 (it ran until February 1888). Its title here is *Sara Crewe; or, What Happened at Miss Minchin's*—a title that indicates the action is as important as the character. Indeed, the story is brief (some 26,000 words), the action abrupt, and the cast of characters small.

Sara Crewe begins with a description of Miss Minchin's Select Seminary for Young Ladies. Sara is already a pupil there, and the narrator quickly gives an analeptic account of her father's bringing her from India and then leaving her with Miss Minchin. By the seventh paragraph of the story, Sara meets with a crisis: the death of her father, her fall into total dependency on Miss Minchin, and her removal to the attic, where she takes up her identity as a maid-of-all-work. In the attic Sara finds comfort in a wax doll, Emily, "who lived in the attic and slept on the iron bedstead at night."[2] Sara is afraid of rats and suffers loneliness as well as fear in her new surroundings. She befriends a "sentimental housemaid" whose popular romances she reads in exchange for doing some of the maid's work, and also a pupil named Ermengarde St. John, who supplies Sara with books of a more improving nature than those she gets from the housemaid. Sara is a strong-willed, even silently aggressive, child whose imagination keeps her from succumbing to the drudgery of her existence at Miss Minchin's.

Imagination also proves efficacious in practical ways. One day as Sara trudges through the wet city streets, she imagines that she finds a sixpence that "belonged to nobody" (*Sara,* 54) and which she spends on six hot buns. Then, in the mud, she finds a fourpenny piece not many paces from a bakeshop. Outside the shop she meets a ragged young girl even worse off than herself. She buys the buns and gives all but one to the beggar child. On her way back to the seminary she imagines things about the Large Family who live in her square, and about the elderly gentleman who lives next door with his *lascar* (servant) from India. Once back at the school, Sara faces the stern figure of Miss Minchin before she is allowed to go to her attic room. Upstairs she opens her door to find that her room has been transformed; it was "warm and glowing" and "seemed changed into fairyland" (*Sara,* 76). Next she receives lots of parcels from a mysterious benefactor.

One night shortly after she receives the parcels, Sara finds the elderly gentleman's monkey in her room. She takes the monkey back to its owner, and the revelation as to her identity and the elderly gentleman's identity takes place. He is the person who was responsible (or so he thinks) for Sara's father's death and loss of fortune in India. He has wanted to find her for a long time, and now he takes her in as her guardian. He asks Sara to call him "Uncle Tom." Explanations occur all around, and Sara becomes friends with the children of Mr. Carmichael, father of the Large Family and lawyer to Uncle Tom. In a final vignette, Sara returns to the bakeshop where she finds the beggar child now employed by the baker-woman.

This story and its potential for character development stayed with Burnett, and in 1902 she saw the first performance of her play *The Little Princess* in London's Avenue Theatre. It opened the following year in New York, at the Criterion. The curtain rises on Sara's eleventh birthday. The school girls dance and sing excitedly in anticipation of Sara's birthday party. Right away Burnett introduces new characters, the schoolgirls Lilly, Lavinia, Jessie, and Lottie. Other girls crowd the stage (including Ermengarde, whom we had met in *Sara Crewe*). Amelia, Miss Minchin's sister, warns the girls against any "rude or unladylike conduct" during the party.[3] Talk of Sara's many presents ensues, and Amelia mentions a doll as one of the presents. When she exits the girls talk of Sara, her father, and India, filling in background for the audience while they play such games as London Bridge.

Miss Minchin then enters, followed by Sara and several servants carrying boxes of presents. One of these servants is Becky, the scullery maid and younger version of the "sentimental housemaid" from *Sara Crewe*. When Sara asks whether Becky may stay for the opening of presents, Miss Minchin declares that "scullery-maids are not little girls—at least they ought not to be" (*Play,* 10). Miss Minchin gives little speeches on deportment, on Sara's fortune, and on the pretty ways she has of thanking the "populace" when they applaud her. Next come the presents, of which the centerpiece is the doll and its finery. Sara speaks of "supposing," comes to Lottie's defense, and then begins to tell the children the beginning of Frances Browne's *Granny's Wonderful Chair*. In the midst of the storytelling, Mrs. Carmichael and her four children, Mazie, Nora, Janet, and Donald, enter. Donald is a rambunctious lad. Everyone is amused at the names Sara has made up for members of the Carmichael family.

At this point a maid enters to announce the arrival of a gentleman from Messrs. Barrow and Skipworth, lawyers. A note also comes for Mrs. Carmichael calling her and her family away because Mr.

Carmichael wants his wife to look in on a Mr. Carrisford who has just landed from India and is very ill. Once Mrs. Carmichael has gone, the children follow a servant to the parlor, where they will have their refreshments. On stage, Miss Minchin greets the lawyer, Barrow. He brings news of Captain Crewe's death and Sara's loss of fortune. As this news is being presented to Miss Minchin and to the audience as well, the voices of the children are heard off stage singing "Here we go round the Mulberry Bush" (*Play,* 26). Amelia goes with orders to tell Sara what has happened, and Miss Minchin discovers Becky, who has been under the table all the time. The first act ends with an interview between Sara and Miss Minchin in which Sara learns that she will have to work for her keep.

Act 2 takes place in Sara's garret room. It opens with Ram Dass, the Indian servant, and a "guest," a white man who tells Ram Dass what to do (the "secretary" in *A Little Princess*), climbing into the room through a window up stage. Plans for the room's transformation are in progress, at Mr. Carrisford's suggestion. Sara comes in when Ram Dass and the guest exit. She speaks of her weariness, apologizes for having no crumbs for a rat she calls Melchisedec (the maneuvering of the rat with wires is described in the stage notes), and addresses her doll. Then Lottie enters to see her "mamma Sara" (*Play,* 35) and to recite her seven times table. Next Ermengarde enters with an armful of books. The conversation between the girls allows Burnett to give information to the audience, regarding the Indian gentleman, his monkey, and Ram Dass. The monkey appears at the window and Sara coaxes him in.

Talk shifts to Sara's hunger, and Ermengarde offers to fetch a box of food that her father had sent to her. A pretend party follows with Ermengarde, Becky, and Sara. They imagine they are at a royal banquet, and Sara plays the part of a minstrel reciting a poem titled "The Little Princess." This poem, which emphasizes the theme of the importance of imagination, does not appear in either *Sara Crewe* or the later novel. Before Sara can finish it, Miss Minchin comes in and ends the party. Left alone, Sara supposes out loud that her room is changed into a beautiful place, warm and snug. Then she sleeps. The audience next watches a dumbshow as Ram Dass and three men bring food, furniture, lamps, and so forth into the room. They remove the old furniture. Sara wakes to find a fire and all the new things about her. The curtain falls on act 2. Then a brief "Recall" takes place with Sara leading Becky into her transformed room. Curtain. Then another recall showing the two girls eating. Then again, this time showing the three girls in the room.

Act 3 takes place in Mr. Carrisford's study. At curtain rise, Ram Dass followed by Donald, Mazie, Nora, and Janet Carmichael enter. Donald rides a tiger's head rug in a boisterous manner while Ram Dass exits to fetch Mr. Carrisford. Much business takes place with the children and Mr. Carrisford when he enters, mostly providing information regarding Sara. Then Mr. Carmichael arrives with no good news regarding his mission, which is to find the little girl of Mr. Carrisford's deceased friend. Ram Dass announces the arrival of Sara, who has come to return the monkey. Of course, identities are revealed. Miss Minchin comes to get Sara, but to her surprise she learns that Sara has a new guardian and a new home. The curtain falls as Sara begins to tell the Carmichael children a story: "Once upon a time, long, long ago—there lived a little Princess—" (68). A recall shows Sara hugging Donald, who stands on the tiger's head.

The success of the play was such that Scribners encouraged Burnett to expand the original story into a full-length novel. The development of *A Little Princess* over 20 years shows Burnett's personal interest in the story. Her interest raises the question as to whether she is completely honest when she says the story is simply "the nice detaily kind of thing children love." The novel offers more than this. It tells the story of a girl who begins life in middle-class comfort, living with her father in India (her mother has died), only to experience sorrow, a fall into extreme adversity, and finally a surprising return to comfort and wealth. That the story is close to Burnett might prompt us to think of it as autobiographical, and Ann Thwaite, Burnett's biographer, is duly prompted: "Sara was undoubtedly Frances herself," she writes.[4]

In what way is Sara a portrait of Frances? As Phyllis Bixler notes in her study *Frances Hodgson Burnett,* Sara is the "fictional sister"[5] of the child Burnett portrays herself to have been in her 1893 memoir,

The One I Knew the Best of All. As a child, Burnett knew both good times and hardship in Manchester; she also attended a day school where she delighted in entertaining her fellow pupils with stories. Indeed, the young Burnett, like Sara Crewe, craved stories; she was, she tells us, "a story-maniac."[6] The imaginations of this real and this fictional child were strong; for example, both developed an intense relationship with a doll. As Burnett puts it in her memoir: "She 'pretends' her doll is somebody out of a story and she is somebody else. She is very romantic" (*Best,* 50). And "romantic," both imaginatively and emotionally, Sara and her creator are. More particularly, Burnett tells us that she possessed, as a "Small Person," "a certain silent steadiness of purpose" coupled with the ability to keep "quiet under some strong emotions" (*Best,* 145). Sara, too, has an intensely emotional yet stoical personality.

This biographical approach, however, can take us only so far. Burnett's own childhood undoubtedly provided some of the feeling for Sara and even hints of some of the novel's action, but the novel is a work of fiction. It relies for inspiration, as all good fiction does, on other fictions. The story of Sara Crewe echoes such fiction as Charlotte Brontë's *Jane Eyre, Villette,* and the unfinished *Emma;* Frances Browne's *Granny's Wonderful Chair;* Matthew Arnold's "The Foresaken Merman"; and the fairy tales "Sleeping Beauty" and "Cinderella." Of these perhaps Brontë's work is the most pervasive in influence on Burnett. The story of an orphan child whose imagination thrives on fairy tales, who experiences hardship and even rejection at school, and who survives to find happiness and fulfillment is repeated in Brontë's works and picked up by Burnett in *A Little Princess.* In developing her plots, Brontë is sharply aware of questions of gender, and this aspect of her work appealed to women writers who followed her in the nineteenth century. Also evident in the novel are allusions to the work of such contemporary writers as George MacDonald, Mary Molesworth, L. T. Meade, and Margaret Gatty. But perhaps most significant is the influence of a book one might not immediately connect with *A Little Princess:* Daniel Defoe's *Robinson Crusoe* (1719). I consider Burnett's novel a reworking of the Crusoe story in terms of female experience; interestingly, four years after publishing *A Little*

Princess, Burnett published an avowedly *Crusoe*-inspired book, *Barty Crusoe and His Man Saturday* (1909). Whereas *Robinson Crusoe* reflects traditional notions of male experience, *A Little Princess* is an attempt to articulate the female counterpart to this experience. The attempt is complicated by a paradox, one that perhaps derives from Burnett's ambivalent feelings toward what the Victorian public knew as "the Woman Question."

The male experience documented in *Robinson Crusoe* is, of course, closely tied in with Britain's colonial expansion. As Martin Green, in *Dreams of Adventure, Deeds of Empire,* has shown, "the adventure tales that formed the light reading of Englishmen for two hundred years and more after *Robinson Crusoe* were, in fact, the energizing myth of English imperialism."[7] This myth admired the pluck, daring, ingenuity, piety, and independence of the British lad. The reckoning went that the British, by virtue of superior development and natural intelligence, were right to assume authority over peoples in various parts of the world. The myth centered on notions of masculine heroism, not least because the imperial stage was the opposite of the domestic one; men went on explorations while women kept the home fires burning. Some women writers, most notably Bessie Marchant, tried to articulate the imperial myth with female heroes. Other writers, however, attempt to write the feminine within the imperial ethos without abandoning the domestic themes and settings of home and homeland. That Burnett's hope is to enter the debate over women's roles within an imperial context is clear from her casual use of India as the starting point for characters such as Mary Lennox and Sara Crewe.

First we need some definition of "the Woman Question." Essentially, the term refers to the intense interest in the role and place of women within British society in the nineteenth century. Many were the competing ideologies debated in the press, in Parliament, in the church, virtually everywhere social debate occurred. That Burnett took an interest in this question of women (how could she not?) is clear from both her private and public writing. In her memoir Burnett tells us that as a young girl she "had great respect for Miss Martineau and Mrs. Ellis and her 'Daughters of England'" (*Best,* 159). These two writers are examples of women who accepted and then defended the inferiority of the female when it came to functioning in the male spheres of business, politics, and warfare. In other words, Burnett learned early on that the woman fulfilled her destiny when she served man as a helpmate, domestic, wife, and mother. Clearly, Burnett took such lessons with a grain of salt. In *The One I Knew the Best of All* she speaks (in the third person) of her relationship with the younger of her two brothers: "As she was only a girl, he despised her in a fraternal British way, but as she was his sister he had a kind of affection for her, which expressed itself in occasional acts of friendly patronage" (*Best,* 36). Just prior to this passage, in a parenthetical aside, Burnett writes, "(Being an English little girl she knew the vast superiority of the male.)" Her irony is nicely apparent.

In her letters, too, Burnett could take an ironic view of "the Woman Question." Thwaite cites a letter of Burnett's to Charles Scribner, written about the time she published *The One I Knew the Best of All,* in which she expresses weariness with the debate concerning women's issues. The context of the letter is a request for copies of some of her books for "the Women's Department of the World's Fair in Chicago." She writes, "I have grown so tired of Woman with a capital W, though I suppose it is rankest heresy to say so. I don't want to be a Woman at all—I have begun to feel that I want to be something like this—'woman.' Neverthless if everybody is sending books, I must send mine" (Thwaite, 149). Being tired of Woman with a capital W does not, however, mean that Burnett was uninterested in the girls and women she wrote about. In *The One I Knew the Best of All* she writes with feeling about the young woman knitting in Islington Square whose brutal father approaches her in an ugly mood. This young woman, she writes, "*was* different" from other young women of her class (*Best,* 73). She had a dignity that moved Burnett later to write the story of Joan Lowrie in the novel *That Lass o' Lowrie's* (1877). The beauty and strength of character she saw in the young woman under the street lamp informs Burnett's fictional female heroes. As Thwaite well puts it, she admired in this woman evidence of "the invincibility of the human spirit, the refusal of women to be mild and submissive, the acceptance of all experience, courage born of adversity. There was certainly no sign that she wanted to write Woman in a small typeface"

(Thwaite, 152). And Burnett herself connects Sara Crewe with another of her creations, the rebellious and fiercely independent Clorinda Wildairs in *A Lady of Quality* (1896). Sara suffered and "was a princess disdaining speech" (quoted in Thwaite, 152).

Burnett, then, did participate in the debate over women's roles, and her position is present in her fiction. *A Little Princess* has much to say about a female's strength of character, her imaginative ability, her ability to learn, her education, and her place within the social order. As in *The Secret Garden* (1911), Burnett's position is ostensibly conservative. She champions the female as nurturer, a dispenser of largesse and a person willing to sacrifice for others, especially for men. The complexity here has to do with Burnett's incorporation and feminine revision of what I think of as the "Crusoe syndrome." The "Crusoe syndrome" is simply the imperial enterprise that was all pervasive in late Victorian England. Indeed, as Edward Said has noted, one did not have to be a conservative to sympathize with England's imperial designs: "With few exceptions, the women's as well as the working-class movement was pro-empire."[8] Burnett's female version of the Crusoe story accepts the imperial myths while it also promotes the woman's cause.

Robinson Crusoe had an immense influence on nineteenth-century children's literature. It set the standard for the boy's adventure story, and it presented a strong argument for Britain's imperialist enterprise. Many are the books that appeared in the nineteenth century telling the story of one or more young men, and sometimes women, marooned on some tropical isle or lost in some barren land where they claim possession of the land through their ability to cultivate it and fashion a garden in the wilderness. Invariably, they also civilize the poor benighted natives with whom they come into contact. Examples of such books are *The Swiss Family Robinson,* by Johann David Wyss (first English version 1814); *Masterman Ready,* by Captain Marryat (1841–42); *The Desert House; or, The English Family Robinson,* by Mayne Reid (1849); *The Island Home; or, The Young Castaways,* by James F. Bowman (1851); *Canadian Crusoes, a Tale of the Rice Lake Plains,* by Catharine Parr Traill (1852); and *The Coral Island,* by R. M. Ballantyne (1857). In the same year *A Little Princess* appeared, so too did *Jumbo Crusoe,* by Ernest Nister, and *Little Miss Robinson Crusoe,* by Mrs. George Corbett. This last indicates the attempt, and not the first, to write a female Robinsonade. Indeed, at the end of the century one of the main challenges for the woman writer, especially one who supported women's rights, was to present successfully the female's role in the expanding British Empire. Because literary convention had emphasized the gentle and passive nature of the female—the so-called angel in the house ideal put forth by Coventry Patmore—the thought of the young woman taking part in dangerous exploration in barbarous lands was not readily countenanced. As Jacqueline Bratton remarks, any encouragement in young girls or women of "independence and self-reliance and the cultivation of physical and mental strength might easily prove subversive, fuelling rebelliousness against the other restrictions of the doctrine of separate spheres."[9] Respected female authors avoided "settings and plots which were directly imperialistic" because the girls' participation in the activities of Empire could only be coarse. This did not, however, mean "that the powerful ideological influence of imperialism was excluded from respectable fiction for girls" (Bratton, 206).

Donald Hall has shown how the imperialistic ethos works its way into domestic fiction. He focuses on the work of Juliana Ewing, especially "Mary's Meadow" (1883), to show how similar it is to *Robinson Crusoe.* The similarity lies in the characters' acquiring "ownership over land through tilling, tending and harvesting someone else's property."[10] The same thing happens, he notes, in Burnett's *The Secret Garden,* in which "an unused space is similarly appropriated and transformed" (Hall, 53). The notion of imperialism set forth in such works is the right of hard-working, reasonable, northern peoples to appropriate land not properly and fully utilized by its inhabitants or previous owners. The values associated with the imperial enterprise are largely masculine: physical labour, reason, aggression, knowledge, adventure. Ewing avoids adventure and aggression to focus on the domestic aspects of the imperial activity, the planting of a garden. The piece of land becomes "Mary's Meadow," ownership signifying the transformation of the land from a wild place into a cultivated one, a point underlined in the story by references to "savages," "niggers," "tom-

toms," and so on. The *Secret Garden* follows this pattern only partially, but then swerves. Mary, with the help of Dickon and Colin, transforms the neglected garden, and in doing so, Hall contends, she "is participating in the same project that her colonial parents did; by exposing the hidden and taming a wild place, she is rendering secure a potentially threatening world" (Hall, 53).

Burnett's engagement with the imperial theme is, however, more complex than this analysis suggests. Hers is a revisionary look at imperialism. True, Mary's parents represent British imperial power, but they are not models the reader admires. They are more interested in power and prestige than in family. Mary must return to England in order to find the ground to fulfill her desire for a garden. In other words, the colonies are not a healthy place for a growing child. Home, family, the English countryside—these are the needful ingredients for a healthy development. The garden at Misselthwaite is not, really, a wild place. It represents motherhood gone to seed. Could Burnett not suggest that the mother (Mary's mother, Colin's mother, the mother-country), indeed motherhood, is likewise dormant and in need of cultivation? The health of the nation depends on the proper cultivation at home, and adventures in the colonies can only result in weakness.

A Little Princess, too, takes up this idea of the weakening effect of the colonies. We learn at the beginning that Sara's father brings his daughter to England because the "climate of India was very bad for children."[11] Later her father's business adventures in India lead directly to his death and to the illness of his friend, Mr. Carrisford. The book ends with no suggestion that either Sara or her guardian, Mr. Carrisford, will return to India. On the other hand, Sara's fortune is a result of those same business adventures that claimed her father's life. Burnett cannot completely escape the imperial ethos of her time. In fact, little Sara is something of a Crusoe at home in that she manages to construct for herself civilized living space in a modern urban wasteland represented by Miss Minchin and her single-minded business practices and by the poverty visible in the London streets. She manages to do this not with the rational, ordered, businesslike acumen of Crusoe himself but with imaginative flare and feminine sympathies. Crusoe becomes "the prince and lord of the whole island" (144) by virtue of his solitary cultivation of the land; Sara, on the other hand, stands out as a natural "princess" because of her natural grace. Whereas *Robinson Crusoe* emphasizes the power of human reason and mechanical construction to fashion a civilized world, *A Little Princess* emphasizes the power of imagination and optimism to transform a dreary world into a wonderful one. Whereas *Robinson Crusoe* moves in the direction of realism, *A Little Princess* moves in the direction of romance.

This distinction between realism and romance is, to a certain extent, artificial. We might discuss Defoe's novel and Burnett's in the context of either realism or romance, since they exhibit both tendencies. To writers and critics in the late Victorian period, however, these two forms were often thought of as separate and each had its champions. The adventure story for boys depended on the fiction of possibility, and to some, as always, the possible and the actual seemed more appropriate for the young than the impossible and fantastic. By century's end, however, fantasy and fairy tale secured a place in children's literature that they have never relinquished. Writers such as Laurence Housman, Oscar Wilde, Mary DeMorgan, Mary Molesworth, Evelyn Sharp, E. Nesbit, and of course Andrew Lang published fairy tales for children. Burnett herself wrote a number of fairy stories. More to the point here, however, is the link some writers forged between fairy tale and the realistic novel. The link is apparent as early as Charles Dickens's *Little Dorrit* (1857–58). Burnett would have also read George MacDonald's *At the Back of the North Wind* (1872), in which young Diamond takes a fantastic voyage to the land behind the North Wind's back and later experiences the streets of London in all their poverty, want, unpleasantness, and even brutality. Later writers, too, would combine the fantastic with the everyday. Obvious examples are Nesbit's *The Five Children and It* (1902) and the two sequels, *The Phoenix and the Carpet* (1904) and *The Story of the Amulet* (1906). Some of H. G. Wells's work also exhibits this conjunction of the real and the fantastic: for example, "The Door in the Wall" (1906) and *The Sea Lady* (1902).

This tendency to conjoin fantasy and reality was an attempt to combat the mechanizing force of scientific discovery, to effect what

Theodore Watts-Dunton termed a "Renascence of Wonder" (the subtitle of his 1898 novel, *Aylwin*). Burnett herself directly addresses this theme in her series of short books for young children beginning with *The Troubles of Queen Silver-Bell* (1907). *A Little Princess* deals with the importance of a belief in wonder less directly, but no less forcefully. Here the setting and action are realistic, but the reader, along with Sara, comes to understand that "magic" does indeed exist. In the context of *A Little Princess,* "magic" is the power of imagination to transform reality. For example, just after Sara has "supposed" that when she is near a bakeshop where they sell hot buns she finds a sixpence, she does in fact find a fourpenny piece just outside a bakeshop. More spectacular still is her imagining the attic room changed from the cold, miserable, and dreary place it is into a warm, comfortable, and elegant room, only to find such a transformation an actuality—overnight in fact. Imagine it and it will happen, the book optimistically says.

To sum up, then, we can see that *A Little Princess* situates itself in several late-Victorian/early-Edwardian themes. Its interest in both social and utopian themes fits the fin de siècle concerns with a socialist encouragement of the poor and with its insistence on esthetic experience as ameliorative. The socialist turn is evident in much of the fairy-tale and fantasy literature written in the late century—works by William Morris, Laurence Housman, Oscar Wilde, and of course Wells. The argument for the beneficial effects of beauty is also evident in writers such as Wilde, Walter Pater, and Andrew Lang. *A Little Princess* contains an argument for charity, a typically Victorian charity, that sees the female as spreading affection and food to the needy, who are also worthy. But in Sara's fall from wealth we learn that the vagaries of economic fortune are fickle, and that even someone in penury might be a princess in spirit. The message is that we need to treat everyone with kindness and encouragement; even someone like the wastrel Anne, who received the bounty of buns from Sara, can become a productive working citizen. On the other hand, the book's insistence on the imagination's power to transform dull reality into the stuff of fairy tale reminds the reader of the importance of esthetic experience. Sara's reading of books results in a transformation of all experience into narrative. As evidenced by her reading of Thomas

Carlyle's *French Revolution,* Sara reads history as if it were fiction. She also perceives life as a story. She herself remarks to Ermengarde, "*Everything's* a story. You are a story—I am a story. Miss Minchin is a story" (109). And the stories most insistent in her mental library are fairy stories.

She even manages to turn the deeds of Empire into the tropes of fairy story. For example, after she first meets Ram Dass, the Indian servant who moves into the house next to Miss Minchin's seminary, his "native costume and the profound reverence of his manner" remind her of her days in India, when she had been "surrounded by people who all treated her as Ram Dass had treated her; who salaamed when she went by, whose foreheads almost touched the ground when she spoke to them, who were her servants and her slaves" (127). In other words, a princess is also a colonial master or mistress. The colonial people, like royal subjects, exist to pay reverence to their mistress; indeed, Ram Dass serves Sara as a sort of fairy-tale helper, bringing her good things anonymously, almost magically. Just as the fairy tale often turns to the "other"—to an animal, a dwarf, or an old crone as the figure of the helper, the one whose magic powers are in the service of the hero—*A Little Princess* incorporates the "other" in the form of this colonial Indian servant to perform magic deeds of service. As the young secretary tells Ram Dass when the two of them survey Sara's room in her absence, the secret transformation of the room "will be like a story from the 'Arabian Nights.'" He adds that "only an Oriental could have planned it" (156).

The backdrop of British imperialism, then, is clear. To this Burnett brings her interest in the role of the female in society. The connection between this interest in the female and Burnett's fascination with the fairy tale is also shaped by history. For much of the Victorian period, the good woman was an "angel": passive, pale, even sickly, but most of all domestic. In short, the connection with the princesses of so many fairy tales—Sleeping Beauty, Snow White, Cinderella, the Goose Girl, and so forth—is direct. Indeed, as others have pointed out, the Cinderella story was of continuous interest to Burnett, and she used it to shape many of her plots. The princess is an ideal devoutly to be wished: obedient, agreeable, dutiful; she exhibits inner beauty. At least ostensibly, Burnett, like such other writers as George MacDonald, was anxious to show that a "princess" was any little girl who exhibited these virtues. For a female to act with sensitivity and grace, politeness and generosity is to act like a princess—in fact, to be a princess.

Another literary context for *A Little Princess* is the school story, usually thought to have begun with the publication of Thomas Hughes's *Tom Brown's School Days* in 1851. Hughes's book inaugurates the boys' school story, but school stories about girls began as early as 1749 with Sarah Fielding's *The Governess; or, Little Female Academy.* In the nineteenth century the girls' school story became popular after 1880 with the publication of many books by L. T. Meade and later followers such as Evelyn Sharp, Evelyn Everett-Green, and Angela Brazil. Burnett's *A Little Princess,* however, does not follow the conventions set out by Meade, in which the reader follows the exploits of a group of schoolgirls through the disruption of school life, the separation of members of the group, and the inevitable restoration of group harmony. Burnett is more interested in following one character, Sara, and taking her through a rite of passage. The trials and tribulations of Sara Crewe, unlike those of Cinderella, who is as sweet at the beginning of the story as she is at the end, produce maturity. As Elizabeth Keyser points out, Burnett "recounts the triumph of emotional honesty over self-deception, active opposition over passive aggression, and acceptance of reality over romantic compensation."[12]

In this context, the book perhaps closest to *A Little Princess* is Mary Molesworth's *The Carved Lions* (1895). The two lions of the title announce the imperial theme. They "had been carved in 'the East,'"[13] a location that might refer to "India or China or Japan." Wherever "East" refers to, Geraldine says, "it might do for fairyland or brownieland" (Molesworth, 8). The colonies, then, are both features of romance and aspects of a very blunt reality. In terms of "reality," England's empire affects Geraldine La Marchant's life similarly to the way it affects Sara's. Geraldine's mother and father leave her behind at Miss Ledbury's school when they depart for South America. Unlike Sara, Geraldine looks forward to school, where she hopes "to have lots of other little girls to play with" (Molesworth, 4). Although their experiences are quite different, both Sara and Geraldine are imaginative girls, and both undergo a fall from innocence at school. In effect, the girls find that, as a foretaste of the wide world, with its interest in the politics of position and power, often based on money, the school is less attractive than the security of the domestic hearth—home and family. What saves both books from promoting a reactionary position regarding a female's role in life is their insistence on the value of a strong will and on resistance to an ungenerous authority.

One difference between the ending of these novels is how each girl's desire receives gratification. *The Carved Lions,* told by Geraldine in the first person, ends with Geraldine an old woman "clinging to a little home of my own" (Molesworth, 144). The book insists on domestic virtues and remains resolutely the chronicle of a private experience. *A Little Princess,* on the other hand, ends with a vision of public activity. Sara takes to the streets to find the little beggar child she had earlier given her hot buns to. She resolves to "give buns and bread to the populace" (296). The book ends with Sara and the beggar child, now working in the bakeshop, sharing a moment of understanding. True, this moment does not wipe clear Burnett's deeply felt sense of class, but it does offer hope for a community of girls across class. In other words, Burnett ends her novel with a vision that goes beyond domesticity and raises questions regarding gender, class, and economic betterment. Sara may have her birth in the nineteenth century, but she will live her adulthood in the twentieth.

2

The Importance of the Work

By placing *A Little Princess* in the context of both the struggle for women's rights and in the general sensibility of Empire, we have touched on two divergent aspects of this book's importance. Both are, to a certain extent, historical. That is, young readers today are unlikely to know the historical circumstances in which this book came into being. This does not mean, however, that the book's importance is either lost on young readers because of their ignorance of history or that the only importance of *A Little Princess* lies in its place in history.

We can argue that the book remains relevant despite the passage of some 90 years since its publication. Although much has happened since 1905 in the area of women's rights, the issues Burnett raises are still worth debating. What kind of education should women have? How does a woman fit into the economic and social structure? Just how are women and girls constructed by our society? How do women relate to one another across class lines? Such questions continue to occupy theorists of women's rights, and that *A Little Princess* raises them is a mark of its claim to our attention. However one articulates the model of female identity set forth in this book—that is, whether one finds the construction of Sara and of the novel's reader reactionary, focusing on such stereotypically feminine traits as emotion, imagination, domesticity, nurturing, and motherhood, or whether one finds it progressive, focusing on such strong characteristics as Sara's acceptance of reality, her social conscience, her stoicism under duress, her resistance to misplaced authority, and her ability and readiness to learn—the fact that the book asks its reader to contemplate female identity and its construction means that it participates in an ongoing dialogue.

The second historical context, the general sensibility of Empire, is also something that continues to occupy us. The age of Empire did not end with World War I. In fact, we continue to deal with aspects of imperial mentality today. What we refer to as "multiculturalism" is a result, in part, of our understanding of just how deeply infected with imperial thinking we are. We cannot read a book such as *A Little Princess* with the same innocence as a reader might have read it in 1905, and it is important to understand just how our experience of cultural diversity differs from that of a reader in 1905. Take, for example, the following passage:

> The sight of his [Ram Dass's] native costume and the profound reverence of his manner stirred all her [Sara's] past memories. It seemed a strange thing to remember that she—the drudge whom the cook had said insulting things to an hour ago—had only a few years ago been surrounded by people who all treated her as Ram Dass had treated her; who salaamed when she went by, whose foreheads almost touched the ground when she spoke to them, who were her servants and her slaves. (127)

This passage holds no irony. The narrator does not comment on the fact that the position Sara is in relative to Miss Minchin and even the cook is not entirely dissimilar to the position Ram Dass and his compatriots are in relative to Sara. Nor does the narrator point out that Sara does not respond to her "masters" with deference the way Ram Dass responds to her. In fact, the book has it both ways: Ram Dass and the other Indian servants are correct in their subservience to

Sara, and Sara in her turn is correct in her resistance to the tyranny of Miss Minchin and her minions. In other words, Burnett never suggests that Ram Dass or his Indian compatriots should resist their roles as acquiescent servants and slaves. The reader of this book in 1905 was unlikely to have even taken notice of this potential irony, but today's reader might well take note of a situation that should be, but isn't, ironic.

Note, too, the introduction of Ram Dass to both Sara and the reader. He emerges from the skylight on Mr. Carrisford's roof, a "picturesque white-swathed form," "dark-faced, gleaming-eyed" and wearing a white turban (124). He is an exotic stranger. He represents one aspect of the "other" against which Sara and her people identify themselves. Throughout the book Ram Dass appears to us as a willing servant, submissive and respectful. We never have the opportunity of knowing him from the inside. He remains a stereotypical figure rather than a character fully realized. In short, he serves Burnett's purpose as a figure of the exotic, the mysterious, the fey. The fact remains, however, that he is a character with a distinct historical and cultural life that is denied him in this novel.

What I am encouraging is the preservation of our past, and this means preserving that which lies silently or unacknowledged in our past. Absent from *A Little Princess* is any consideration of the historical and cultural significance of Ram Dass and his compatriots; but rather than neglect what is absent, we would do well to recall the book's contexts—the cultural and historical circumstances that lurk just beyond the borders of what Burnett writes. To read a book such as *A Little Princess* is to keep the dialogue with history going. It is important to know just how society, through its literature, constructed both a sense of self and other, and a sense of gender. Young readers today have the opportunity to compare the contemporary social construction of gender and race with that at the turn of the century. This calls for, of course, critical reading—that is, reading that engages with the text thoughtfully rather than reading for plot alone.

Reading for plot alone, however, is not necessarily something we need to discourage altogether. The importance of *A Little Princess,* or any book for that matter, does not lie solely in its historical context.

Two other perspectives on reading give us more to say regarding the book's importance: the first is a traditional thematic reading, and the second is formal. In other words, we can argue that what the book has to say is important, and so, too, is its esthetic or literary form. The focus on one or the other of these perspectives will depend on whether we have an interest in the ethics of reading or in a more formal literary competence.

From a thematic perspective, we might wish to emphasize Burnett's interest in the power of imagination, what we now think of as the power of positive thinking. Anne Thwaite informs us that in the early 1880s Burnett became "interested in mind healing" and its expression in Christian Science. In 1884 she took treatments from a mind-healer in Boston. What all this amounted to was a belief that the mind could make things happen, especially things associated with the body. We can see this belief at work in *The Secret Garden* in Colin's desire to get well and his consequent improvement in health. In *Sara Crewe* and later *A Little Princess,* Sara's determination not to despair and her optimistic game of supposing make her life tolerable. By pretending she is a prisoner in the Bastille or by pretending to have a feast when Ermengarde brings her basket of goodies, Sara transforms a life of drudgery into something less dreadful. She gains a measure of control over her life, thereby thwarting Miss Minchin's spiteful attempt to make her suffer. The book champions imaginative activity.

By calling this imaginative activity "magic," Burnett manages to do something else: she invests her world with spirit. As in *The Secret Garden,* where "magic" clearly signifies a spiritual power, in fact the spiritual power of the Christian God, in *A Little Princess* "magic" betokens a divine presence that takes care of little princesses, those who believe in good things. The transformation of Sara's attic room into a splendidly comfortable place is carried out by Ram Dass, under orders from Mr. Carrisford. These two act as dei ex machina, taking care of the beautiful child who so badly needs and deserves their protection. The message is familiar to readers of children's books: the world may appear dreadful, but hope is never misplaced since reality is always good. The world is, despite occasional appearances to the contrary, made for little children.

The other side of the coin, so to speak, gives us Miss Minchin. Here is a person whose value system is intricately connected to the economic system. She is most interested in making money, and this lust for the almighty guinea turns her into something of a witch. She is obsequious when she thinks she can make money from Sara's father and from Sara's presence in her academy as the star pupil. But she is spiteful and even cruel once she learns that Sara's father has died and left her no fortune, not even a modest one. Her comeuppance comes, of course, on the revelation of Sara's identity to Mr. Carrisford. Sara does have a fortune, but Miss Minchin will not get her mitts on it. Miss Minchin is a businesswoman who puts all her energy into her business. She is also a person who carries a grudge; ever since Sara's first French lesson, Miss Minchin has secretly harbored ill feelings toward her pupil. As a result of both her greed and her ungenerous nature, she suffers loss of relationship and emotional security. She suffers from what Burnett terms her "worldly folly" (283).

As for Sara, she receives the bounty of her father's diamond mines and the warmth of Mr. Carrisford's home. She is rewarded for her virtue, which we might define as optimism and care for others. Sara has acted as mother to Lottie, friend to Becky, tutor to Ermengarde, and benefactor to the beggar child she meets on the London streets. Despite her own woes, she has remained cheerful and thoughtful. Her story is familiar, based as it is on "Cinderella." From the beginning, children's books have expressed this moral: the person who is dutiful, resourceful, and kind will triumph in the end. *A Little Princess* has much in common with *The History of Little Goody Two-Shoes* (1767).

Mention of "Cinderella" and *Little Goody Two-Shoes* reminds us of the formal importance of *A Little Princess.* Not only is this novel important historically, for its conflation of romance with realism (a conflation evident in other Burnett books), but also for its presentation of character. Unlike many of the child charcters in children's books up to the early twentieth century, Sara Crewe is not one-dimensional. In this she differs from such characters as Kate Caergwent in Charlotte Yonge's *Countess Kate* (1862), Katy Carr in Susan Coolidge's "Katie" series (1872–73), and Rebecca Randall in Kate Douglas Wiggin's

Rebecca of Sunnybrook Farm (1903). What makes Sara Crewe different from these other female characters is her distinctly rebellious nature. She has passion, and passion that can burst out uncontrollably. For example, before her fall from material comfort, Sara finds herself called on to defend Lottie against the bullying of an older girl, Lavinia. While reading about the French Revolution one day, Sara hears Lavinia remark about Lottie: "Nasty, little spoiled thing, I should like to *slap* her!" (58). Sara gets up from her chair and says "with some fire, 'I should like to slap *you*—but I don't want to slap you . . . and I should *like* to slap you—but I *won't* slap you'" (59). The narrator admits that Sara "was not an angel" (59), reminding us just how her character differs from the standard Victorian "angel in the house."

Even more telling is Sara's defiance when Miss Minchin informs her of her father's death and her own dependent position. She tells Miss Minchin that she is "*not* kind" and that her school is "*not* a home" (83). Her father once remarked that if Sara had been born a boy and lived a few centuries ago, then "she would have gone about the country with her sword drawn, rescuing and defending every one in distress" (27). She defends Lottie, Becky, and herself from the meanness of others. She is not all sweetness and light; she has "a fine, hot little temper" (27).

But what about this makes the book "important"? And for whom do we speak when we consider the book's importance? Obviously, the story was important to Burnett; she wrote and rewrote it over a 20-year period. Sara's passion for reading, her ability to tell stories, and her "certain silent steadiness of purpose when she meant to do a thing" (*Best,* 145) reflect aspects of Burnett's own personality. Also, the fantasy of a child finding that he or she is special—a little princess or a lord—was dear to Burnett, and might stem from her own somewhat difficult and financially insecure childhood. That a book is important to its author is, however, no reason for saying it is important for its readers. I have touched on several historical and literary reasons for making such a claim, but perhaps an even stronger case can be made for the book's psychological importance for young readers.

As the title indicates, Burnett had fairy tales in mind when she wrote this book. At the very least, we have romance—that is, wish fulfillment—in *A Little Princess.* The book fits Bruno Bettelheim's thesis that fantasy serves a comforting role for the young reader by presenting her with the consolation of difficulty overcome. Sara, like such fairy-tale characters as Hansel and Gretel, the Goose Girl, or Cinderella, finds herself without the protection and comfort of a mother or father and forced to be independent. Rather than despair, Sara copes with her difficult situation and even finds a small community of friends. By facing her problems squarely, she overcomes them. Instead of a fairy godmother, Sara has a secret godfather who ensures her comfort and safety. The message here is that a well-ordered psyche has the protection of a strong superego. Whether one wishes to read the character of Mr. Carrisford as a sign of a divinely ordered universe or a healthy and unified psyche, the book offers reassurance to the young reader that, faced forthrightly, the world is not a place to fear.

In short, *A Little Princess* offers the reader the three ingredients of fantasy outlined first by J. R. R. Tolkien and later repreated by Bettelheim: recovery, escape, and consolation. The reader recovers a green world through a reading of the novel. By this I mean that the book delivers a vision of reality that asks the reader to return to his or her own world refreshed, ready to see the world again, not for the first time, since this is impossible, but with a renewed sensitivity. For example, the reader might look again at her dolls and experience something of the thrill of belief in their powers of animation that Sara feels. As for escape, this does not mean escape to a fantasy world without any connection to the world the reader inhabits outside her reading but, rather, an escape to a world where magic works—not the kind of magic performed by a conjuror but the magic of belief, the magic of transformation made possible by imaginative activity.

Finally, consolation, a feeling that a golden world does in fact wait for the person who suffers through life's tribulations, delivers hope to the characters in the novel and to the reader. Sara not only finds herself rescued from the trials of living as Miss Minchin's drudge but herself rescues others from their lives of drudgery. She plans to "give buns and bread to the populace" (222), thereby offering them consolation. The reader, in Bettelheim's paraphrase of Tolkien, gains "the confidence that, despite all [the] tribulations he has to suffer . . . not only will he succeed, but the evil forces will be done away with and never again threaten his peace of mind."[14] *A Little Princess* ends with a moment of understanding and connection—physical as well as psychological—between Sara and Anne as their hands grip and their eyes meet. This vision of connection between girls of differing socioeconomic spheres offers hope for the future, hope for a community of women based on mutual understanding.

3

Critical Reception

In the first number of the journal for girls, *Atalanta,* Augustine Birrell notices in his "Notes about Books" Frances Hodgson Burnett's "new book," *Sara Crewe and Editha's Burglar.* What strikes him is the book's "sentiment," something he also finds in *Little Lord Fauntleroy.* What differentiates the two books, however, is the character of the eponymous heroes. Birrell makes it clear that he prefers Sara to Cedric Errol: "to do her justice she is by no means so good a little girl as was his lordship a good boy; she displays a good deal of temper, which her miserable circumstances certainly excused."[15] Finally, though, he can only disparage sentiment and suggest a reading of Burnett's *Louisiana* (1880) as a bracing antidote to *Faunterloy* and *Sara Crewe.* What is interesting about this early review of Burnett's story is the reviewer's distinction between the popularity of sentiment and the sublimity of "pathos." In other words, Birrell's thesis anticipates that of Phyllis Bixler in a work published nearly one hundred years later. For Bixler, *Fauntleroy* marks a watershed in Burnett's writing, effecting a shift in Burnett from a serious novelist to a popular one.

The notice of *Sara Crewe* in *Atalanta* is thin, commenting on Sara's character and then sketching the plot. I note from the advertisement pages bound into the back of Burnett's *The Captain's Youngest, Piccino, and Other Child Stories* (1894) snippets from two other reviews of *Sara Crewe.* From the *Morning Post* we have praise for the "artistic and delightful" story, and from the *Spectator,* we have this: "As an idealized portrait of a child who makes a wretched life not only endurable, but positively enjoyable, by living it in a world of pure imagination, *Sara Crewe* is perfect." Perhaps most noteworthy in the subsequent history of this book's critical reception (and the same is true of *A Little Princess*) is how little attention it receives from critics. The history of the book's reception offers a lesson (if we needed one) of the fortunes of a popular story: neglected in the critical reviews and read avidly by the general reader. By implication, this story speaks to a readership both old and young, a common feature of popular literature. With this in mind, we might note Burnett's subtitle to her stage version of this story: "A Play for Children and Grown-Up Children in Three Acts." Given this broad appeal of the story, critics are, perhaps, disarmed; they do not know where to place the book. Consequently, they ignore it. Also, if the book appeals to such a broad readership, then it cannot have a profound message concerning the human condition.

Reviews of the longer novel, *A Little Princess,* are positive but skimpy. Although such periodicals as the *Saturday Review* and *Illustrated London News* did review children's books, neither contain mention of Burnett's novel. The *Bookman,* in its Christmas Supplement of 1905, referred to *A Little Princess* as "this touching and spirited story," and suggested that the ending of Sara's "time of child-grief" is "quite in keeping with the requirements of Christmas."[16] This same number, however, contains a lengthy article by Thomas Seccombe, "Classics of the Nursery; or, The Development of Books for Boys and Girls" (120–27), which mentions none of Burnett's books. Also in this number appears a chart of the best-selling books in 36 British cities: Burnett's name appears on this list 12 times, in one-third of the cities.

The *Athenaeum,* a sturdy minder of the nation's cultural health, has little to say regarding *A Little Princess,* except to point out that for an author "to tell a story three times" is unusual, although "all three versions are charming."[17] The reviewer thinks Sara must be "one of the most beloved of the author's dream-children." The use of the term "dream-children" hints at the ideal nature of Burnett's heroes and might also remind us of Augustine Birrell's charge of "sentiment" in relation to Cedric Errol and Sara Crewe. But these comments, like the ones in the *Bookman* and the *Spectator,* are cursory. Their very brevity and descriptive tone suggest that the reviewers were not deeply affected by Burnett's book.

"Charming," a word that appears in the *Athenaeum,* also turns up in the *Spectator,* which refers to the book as "very charming." The story, the review goes on to say, "is admirably managed by Mrs. Burnett, who contrives with her Indian Gentleman and his servant Ram Dass to give a touch of the 'Arabian Nights' to her tale. Ram Dass is quite of the good-genie kind."[18] This is the only mention of the imperial theme in the reviews of the book I have found, and here it is transmuted into a safe "faerie" realm: the "Arabian Nights." The reviewer divests Ram Dass of any vestige of humanity he might have had by comparing him to the "good-genie kind." The "charm" of the book, apparently, lies in its cute handling of the Indian gentleman and his servant. The reader does not reflect on the implications of British superiority and the imperial enterprise because he or she is charmed by romance. This, with the exception of Lynne Schwartz's Afterword to the 1990 Signet edition of the novel, is the closest that any commentary on the story, either then or even now in the 1990s, comes to uncovering the imperial theme.

Little consideration of *A Little Princess* appears in the academic treatment of children's books until quite recently. As Elaine Showalter says in *A Literature of Their Own,* Burnett is best known for *Little Lord Fauntleroy* and *The Secret Garden.*[19] *A Little Princess* receives just passing mention in the standard histories of children's literature, and no mention at all in such early works as Annie E. Moore's *Literature Old and New for Children* (1934) and Geoffrey Trease's *Tales Out of School* (1949). Roger Lancelyn Green, in *Tellers of Tales* (1946), refers to it as "an enthralling wish-fulfillment story for children."[20] In 1950, however, Marghanita Laski began to give the book its due (despite getting the title incorrect by calling it *The Little Princess*) when she wrote that it "has the extraordinary faculty of adapting itself to the mental needs of the child reader so that it can be enjoyed, at different levels, for a surprising range of years."[21] Laski praises the book as evidence that Burnett "has moved far beyond the simple sentiments of *Little Lord Fauntleroy*" (Laski, 86). Burnett is successful in arousing the child reader's emotions and bringing them to a satisfying resolution. Laski's interest is in the book's appeal to its readership, and she offers no thematic, formal, or psychological analysis.

For this we have to wait until the 1970s and after. As a prelude to a more analytical approach to *A Little Princess,* we have Isabelle Jan's provocative comments in *On Children's Literature* (1969; trans. 1974). Jan considers Burnett's book in the context of changing social conditions, and her remarks suggest Burnett is a reactionary writer, one accepting the reigning ideology of late-nineteenth-century bourgeoise life. In her chapter on "The Home," Jan (who also mistitles the novel) argues that such heroes as those in *A Little Princess* "experienced poverty isolated from its social context."[22] By isolating the poor child figure "from any distinct environment" (Jan, 97), the writer can reassure the child reader that all will be well, while at the same time offering no explicit criticism of social conditions. What Jan would make of the beggar child Anne remains conjecture, since she does not consider her in the discussion. Jan's focus on social issues is fruitful, but the approach does not attract other researchers to Burnett's work.

A more influential reading of *A Little Princess* comes in the ground-breaking book by Mary Cadogan and Patricia Craig, *You're a Brick, Angela!* (1976). They note the pervasive influence of the "Cinderella" story on Burnett's work, but they do not see this as a strength. Despite the fact that Cadogan and Craig categorize Burnett's work as sentimental and conservative, they place her in the context of women's writing effectively drawing attention to Burnett's attitudes to women and girls. Their criticism of Burnett's acceptance of class, and their observation that at the end Becky, "though an equal partner with Sara in the days of drudgery and semi-starvation at Miss Minchin's, does not become a 'sister' to the Little Princess, but her 'delighted attendant'—in other words, her maid,"[23] is not flattering, but it does direct the reader's attention to issues concerning the female, sisterhood, and society.

In 1978 Phyllis Bixler published the first of many articles and a book on Burnett; the first piece is "Tradition and the Individual Talent of Frances Hodgson Burnett: A Generic Analysis of *Little Lord Fauntleroy, A Little Princess,* and *The Secret Garden.*" As this title indicates, Bixler's focus is on the relation of Burnett's books to genres of children's literature; she shows how *A Little Princess* combines the fairy tale and the exemplum. Six years after the publication of this study, Bixler's major work on Burnett appeared in Twayne's English Authors Series. Here Bixler treats *A Little Princess* as a "Cinderella" variant. Unlike Cadogan and Craig, however, Bixler sees the use of the fairy-tale plot as a strength of the novel. She admires the book for its "mature craftsmanship" (1984, 90) and for the complexity of Sara's character. She also focuses on the theme of imagination as it manifests itself in Sara's belief in "magic." A year after publishing *Frances Hodgson Burnett,* Bixler contributed the entry on Burnett in *American Writers for Children before 1900,* volume 42 of *The Dictionary of Literary Biography.* Whereas the very placement of Burnett in this volume indicates her Victorian sensibility and suggests she was not a modernist, we would do well to remember that she published 22 books after 1900. Bixler reprises her earlier comments on *A Little Princess* but adds a brief comparison of the three forms of the story; this is the first attempt to show the development Burnett brought to the story.

Two themes mentioned in the previous paragraph receive greater notice in the next couple of years. In 1987 Juliet Dusinberre, in *Alice to the Lighthouse,* takes up the issue as to whether Burnett's sensibility is Victorian or modernist. She discusses Burnett in the context of late-nineteenth-century children's books and ideas concerning children.[24] As the nineteenth century turned into the twentieth, notions of the child's place changed dramatically, and the new spaces opened to children in the world outside the nursery are reflected in literature written for and about children. A book such as *A Little Princess,* Dusinberre argues, uses children to criticize adult values. And Sara's very need for narrative and her awareness of its ubiquity point forward to Virginia Woolf's *The Waves* (1932).

Bixler's brief comparison of the three versions of Sara's story is somewhat developed by Marian E. Brown in her article "Three

Versions of *A Little Princess:* How the Story Developed" (1988).[25] I say "somewhat" because this article is not especially helpful. For example, the stage version is neither quoted nor documented. The effect of compression or expansion is not dealt with. The staging of Ram Dass's transformation of Sara's attic room is quite different, for practical reasons having to do with stagecraft, from the same incident in the novel. Burnett develops the Carmichael children quite differently from the way she develops them in the novel; young Donald is especially interesting. Brown does point out major changes such as the inclusion of Sara's befriending a rat or her telling what is obviously the beginning of Frances Browne's fantasy, *Granny's Wonderful Chair,* in the play version. Having said this, I hasten to add that more work on the various versions of the story needs to be done.

Perhaps the best interpretive account of *A Little Princess* is Elizabeth Keyser's "'The Whole Story': Frances Hodgson Burnett's *A Little Princess,*" which appeared in 1986. Keyser is the first critic to point out that the book contains an ambivalence toward romance. She sees that Burnett's attachment to storytelling and the imagination is not without its darker side; that is, she points out that the romantic imagination may be dangerous. The attic in which Sara performs her imaginative storymaking, Keyser notes, is itself a trope for the imagination, but its very dreariness should be a warning to the reader. Rather than deceive oneself by imagining that things are other than they are, one is far better to accept reality. Implicit in Keyser's approach is a sociological, as well as a psychological, point. Sara is not only emotionally healthy at the end of the book, not needing to rely on a doll for support, but she also sees clearly social ills and the need for amelioration. Her final story is about Anne, the beggar girl, and in it she "acknowledges both the sordid facts of Anne's existence and Sara's kinship with and responsibility for her" (Keyser, 242).

This last point—Sara's perception of the needs of others—returns us to notions of motherhood. After all, Sara's desire to feed bread to the populace is an extension of her eagerness to serve as Lottie's mother. The point is developed at length in Phyllis Bixler's "Gardens, Houses, and Nurturant Power in *The Secret Garden*" (1991). As the title indicates, this essay deals with Burnett's most enduring children's book, but it also offers comment on *A Little Princess.* Bixler's interest is in the evocation of the mother and mothering in Burnett's works. She adopts the notion of the secret mysteries of the mother's body voiced in women's writing (or in some women's writing) to account for the power of nature and the garden in *The Secret Garden.* In *A Little Princess* the nurturant power of nature passes from images of the mother to images of the father, and we have such nurturing males as Sara's father, Mr. Carmichael, Ram Dass, and Mr. Carrisford. Indeed, the possible mother figures here are blocked from expressing nurturing power either by a desire for money (Miss Minchin) or by weakness of will (Amelia). Bixler concludes that in "Burnett's utopia . . . neither nurturant nor economic power would be the province of one gender; men would nurture and women would own houses."[26]

In all of this, we see a continuing interest in the fairy-tale aspects of *A Little Princess,* some attention to the story's social implications, a nod in the direction of women's writing, and nothing in the way of placing the book in the context of the fiction of Empire. Two exceptions to this last point are Juliet Dusinberre, who does, in passing, bring together the two texts I compare in chapter one, *A Little Princess* and *Robinson Crusoe,* and Lynne Sharon Schwartz, who, in her Afterword to the 1990 Signet edition of the novel, notes that Burnett wrote her novel "in an era of colonialism." She goes on to say that the book's "condescension toward India in general and Ram Dass in particular—exotic, charming, but unquestionably fated for dominion by the white man—is no longer acceptable."[27] In writing about the impact of Defoe's book in the late nineteenth century, Dusinberre notes that "like Frances Hodgson Burnett's Sara Crewe, [Defoe] had used the story [of his own life] to transform a different kind of desert island" (Dusinberre, 228). Sara, we recall, uses her own unfortunate situation as the basis for her stories of life in the Bastille. But again, Dusinberre's focus is not on the theme of Empire. This theme, among others, will occupy us in the next section, a reading of *A Little Princess.*

First, however, I ought to acknowledge Schwartz's commentary, as it offers a distinctly personal voice to the academic voices I have chronicled. Schwartz begins her essay on *A Little Princess* by confessing her "need" for this book. She regularly returns to it "as some people need to revisit a beloved landscape or hear a certain piece of music from time to time" (223). The book, she says, holds a "crucial bit of knowledge." For Schwartz, this knowledge gave her the patience to "wait until my inner vision could find its way into the actual world" (224). In other words, Burnett's theme of self-identity or imaginative belief—Sara's insistence in perceiving herself a "princess"—speaks to Schwartz; it gives her something personal and inalienable. This approach allows Schwartz to focus on something often neglected in readings of the novel: the power invested in children. Sara's power derives from the very thing her culture demands of her: silence and patience. Sara's refusal to break down in front of Miss Minchin, her generally stoic demeanor, distresses Miss Minchin, making her feel "as if her might was being set at nought" (82).

Schwartz does not couch her commentary in overtly feminist language, but the importance of her response to the book is its clear indication that *A Little Princess* can, after 90 years, still speak powerfully to a female reader of the necessity of speaking stories. When I mentioned that Sara's silence is a means of her asserting power, I did not mean to rule out the reverse situation: Sara's storytelling. Sara is silent in the face of authority figures, those who desire to dominate her, but she is willing to speak volumes to those interested in story. For Schwartz, this storying is of central importance. She responds to Sara's eager assertion that "*Everything's* a story" this way: "Story within story, world without end. We make up our own as we go along. And since it is all a story, how much better to make it up for ourselves than to let the world make it up for us" (225).

A READING

4

A Response to *A Little Princess*: Female Empowerment

What follows is a short essay I wrote in January 1993 as part of an assignment in my children's literature class. The instructions were to write a personal response to *A Little Princess* without feeling the necessity of commenting on anything formal or academic. I was the class instructor but took part in the response assignments with the students. One other thing: my response followed my first reading of the book. Previously, I had only read two of Burnett's works: *Fauntleroy* and *The Secret Garden*. My title for the brief essay was "Speaking from the Endpapers: An Anonymous Review of *A Little Princess*." Here is the essay.

My copy of *A Little Princess* (the Puffin reprint of 1973) has an inscription inside the front cover written in a child's hand: "This is an excellent book!" I have no idea who wrote this or when the person wrote it. I purchased the book for 30 cents in a secondhand bookshop several years ago. Since the paperback edition that contains this inscription has a publication date of 1973 and I have owned it for at least 10 years, I must conclude that the child's hand dates from sometime in the 1970s. But what does such a conclusion have to say to adults who consider this book in the 1990s? What I wish to meditate on are the implications of this anonymous voice speaking from the endpapers of my copy of *A Little Princess.*

First, I reiterate that I cannot know who wrote the inscription. That the person was a child seems evident to me from the quality of the handwriting. The person writes; he or she does not print, but the handwriting is careful to the point of inexperience. I note, too, that the inside blurb indicates that the book is "mainly for girls of eight to twelve." From this I take the plunge and suspect that the person writing the inscription was female. If I am right, then what have I learned? If nothing else, I have evidence that a book first published as long ago as 1905 could still attract readers (or at least one reader) in the 1970s. We live in a time when the past is often allowed to collect dust—recently one of my students remarked that a film she had seen wasn't much good because it was in black and white—and we are generally preoccupied with the here and now as if the here and now's existence did not depend on the past.

But what about this book prompted someone to write in it "an excellent book"? On the level of plot, *A Little Princess* has the elements familiar to us from fairy tale. This is the story of the trials and tribulations of a well-to-do young girl who falls into poverty and disgrace (sort of), suffers ill treatment at the hands of a mother surrogate, and finally escapes from poverty through the offices of a kindly next-door neighbor. This is a "Cinderella" story. A combination of the girl's own strengths of character and assistance from above (Ram Dass enters the attic through the skylight) leads to the happy ending. But nothing of this is particularly new. What prompted the absent hand to give this book its imprimatur?

I suppose we could fall back on familiar ideas. We could say that Burnett's book has a strong sense of place, Miss Minchin's academy being fairly well described. We might comment on the presentation of characters and remark that Sara might attract readers with her imaginative ways, her ingenuous nature, her strength of spirit, and her affection for others. We might consider the reference to India and the monkey next door as touches of the exotic. We might look to the portrayal of the imaginative life of children—I refer to Emily and Melchisedec—as strong and sure to attract young readers, just as it does in *Anne of Green Gables*. We might refer to the aura of romance Burnett gives her book, something that has charmed adult readers as well as children in book after book, decade after decade. By romance, I mean the book's presentation of desire. Romance offers wish-fulfillment, and what could be more fulfilling to a child reader than the sense that fathers will not abandon children? I might as well speak forthrightly. I sense in Burnett a privileging of the father, a yearning for the father. Little Sara obviously has a strong relationship with the father who leaves her at Miss Minchin's. He, however, is young and naive and sentimental. What Sara needs is a stronger father figure, someone who, like herself, has experienced the bracing winds of adversity. Consequently, by the end of the story she has this father figure in the person of Mr. Carrisford.

Perhaps this fairy-tale quality to the book can capture young readers. But I doubt that this alone accounts for the success of *A Little Princess* with our absent reader. For one thing, the whole "princess" motif rings false to me. First, we are to take the word *princess* as a metaphor. We have seen this before in George MacDonald, and perhaps in Lewis Carroll's *Through the Looking-Glass*. Clearly, Sara Crewe is not literally a princess. Her father treats her as one by spoiling her. She gets everything she wants and more; she has been waited on hand and foot in India. But Burnett's point is that such spoiling has not adversely affected this child; she remains in a positive sense "the little friend of all things" (153): children who can't learn, destitute children, monkeys, Indian servants, rats, and dolls. In other words, we have here a princess of a child—good through and through, naturally good.

Let's look at this state of perfection. I notice that Sara Crewe likes things she can dominate, starting with her father. The best metaphor for this desire for domination is Sara's relationship with her doll. Emily's function in the story is ostensibly to illustrate Sara's imagination; here is a little girl who can even imagine that her doll is alive. But Sara wants to believe her doll *is* alive, and she treats her with the same degree of condescension she brings to everyone else. Once I note this, I note that Sara likes to take charge; she likes to be in a position of superiority. She patronizes both Ermengarde and Becky. Late in the story she does the same to the street urchin, Anne. In fact, the story ends on this note of condescension when the restored Sara confers on the once wastrel Anne the honor of giving fresh buns to other street kids. What I detect here is a real imperial attitude.

Most young readers would like to assume vicariously (and probably actually) positions of dominance in their social relationships. *A Little Princess* gratifies this desire.

Much of this is unpalatable to me, and I can only find solace in the possibility of another kind of empowerment to be found in these pages. I speak of Sara's storytelling ability. Sara speaks. Unlike Mary Lennox in *The Secret Garden,* Sara does not fade from view in the final third of the book. In fact, the last thing we see is Sara visiting Anne in the bakeshop to offer charity to the downtrodden. One thing might ring from these pages: a girl is not helpless, silent, entirely dependent, and necessarily subservient. Girls can survive on their own merits and using their own wits.

Such were my thoughts after my first reading of the book. My discussion shows no clear understanding of the imperial background to the story, although a hint of this theme does appear in what I wrote. You can, however, see that female empowerment interested me then as it does now. Even my focus on the inscription in my paperback edition concerns a female voice and its delight in this book. But I was not confident in my assessment of the book's depiction of the female. Sara might have inner strength and she might show defiance in the face of Miss Minchin's tyrannical authority, but early in the book these strengths appear the strengths of a soldier. Sara remarks to her father that she does not like the look of Miss Minchin's academy; she adds that "soldiers—even brave ones—don't really *like* going into battle" (11). She implies that she, too, is a soldier, and that her time at the academy will be a battle, as indeed it is—a battle of wits and wills. Later, when Sara tells Ermengarde how much she misses her father, she adds that she will endure the pain of his absence: "You have to bear things. Think what soldiers bear!" (33). Again, she speaks of herself, at least by implication, as a soldier. In other words, Sara's stoicism is a mark of her affinity with male values, and we might argue that she learns to put such male traits behind her when she finally cries. After her outburst of sobs in chapter 10, the central chapter, Sara comes to know of Ram Dass and the "Indian Gentleman" next door; in other words, once she has allowed her female tears full vent, her guardian male appears on the scene.

Still, this interpretation of Sara's male and female characteristics does not take into account her nurturing instincts. She not only serves as a "mother" to Lottie, but she also offers bread to the populace. Sara impresses others with her generous nature. Although Burnett does not take her into adulthood, we know by the end of the book that Sara is not strictly domestic and house-bound. She does serve as Mr. Carrisford's "companion," but she also convinces him to allow her to "give buns and bread to the populace" (298), suggesting she has interests beyond the domestic sphere. A female economy, the book seems to suggest, would be quite different from the male economy accepted by Miss Minchin and those like her. In fact, we might argue that the male economy—one that takes an interest in speculation and diamond mines—is directly involved in Captain Crewe's death and Mr. Carrisford's illness. Sara comes as an antidote to the desire for filthy lucre, and her understanding of money is that it can serve others and not only the self.

My thinking about the book's attitudes toward female identity and social role took a deeper tone from the work of my former student and now colleague Mavis Reimer. In her Ph.D. dissertation, "Tales Out of School: L. T. Meade and the School Story," Reimer discusses *A Little Princess* in the context of the school story. She points out that Sara's imaginative power, her ability to make a story out of nearly everything, is not a sign of female empowerment. As she puts it, "Sara's ability to make a story of the world is not the power to make the world, . . . but only the power to forget the world."[28] Sara's remarkable gift of imagining and pretending things "until she almost believed them" (*A Little Princess,* 28) *prepares* her for the marvelous things that will happen in her life, but it does not *make* those things happen.

But as Reimer also notes, Sara has "for some time" been working "to make herself visible to the 'Indian gentleman'" (Reimer, 104). She feels sorry for him and often stands outside his house sending her good wishes to him and hoping he feels "a little warm and comforted," without knowing why. She has designs to make the gentleman feel in better health. These designs come to pass when the gentleman comes to know the truth of Sara's identity. As Reimer notes, drawing on the work of Nancy Armstrong, Sara succeeds in "transforming the male from a competitive brute into a benevolent father" (105).[29] Mr. Carrisford's competitive instincts have been broken, however, before Sara comes into his life. Carrisford feels remorse for having something to do with Captain Crewe's death, and he feels responsible for the little girl he has never met. In other words, Carrisford is predisposed to act as father to Sara before he ever meets her. Sara, like the characters in fairy tales, simply receives the bounty that comes her way; she does not make any of it happen despite her desire to do so. She is, finally, a passive character. In her passivity, she does not offer a revisionary version of the fairy-tale princess in the way, for example, that characters created by Burnett's comtemporaries Evelyn Sharp and E. Nesbit do.

To find a feminist message in this novel, as Bixler has implicitly argued, is to look to the power of the nurturing spirit. One aspect of this nurturing spirit essential to female empowerment is Sara's storytelling gift. However ineffectual her pretending may be in transforming the world, it does give her an identity among her schoolmates; it gives her a way of speaking about and coping with her dread, and it allows her imaginative sympathy with the "populace." In terms of the book's plot and characters, the "populace" Sara feels drawn to are the marginalized schoolgirls Lottie and Ermengarde, the lower-class servant girl Becky, and the street urchin Anne. Not only are these characters on the fringe of society—those considered the "other" by the dominant members of the social group—but they are also all girls. In other words, Burnett shows, however incipiently, the importance of girls befriending girls both within and across social class. This focus on coping in isolation (Sara's imaginative survival in her attic room) and on the formation of support groups (Sara and her school friends and her friendship with Anne) make the book well worth reading 90 years after its publication.

5

The Cult of the Child: From Seven to Eleven

The formation of a group or community takes place around a center. In other words, as fin de siècle uncertainties affected many of Burnett's contemporaries from Wilde to Wells, Burnett herself remained strongly attached to the certainties of the century's romantic ethos. We might recall that Sara Crewe speaks French as, quite literally, her mother-tongue (her mother was a "Frenchwoman" [22], and since the beginning of the nineteenth century France had been associated with liberty, equality, and fraternity). From France, too, came many of the ideas about children and their education. In England, the early nineteenth century saw the apotheosis of the child as a sage and seer blessed in William Wordsworth's famous "Ode on the Intimations of Immortality" (1805). Throughout the century, in works by Dickens, George MacDonald, Charles Kingsley, Lewis Carroll, George Eliot, and others, the Wordsworthian child continued to perpetuate essentialist notions of human purity and natural goodness.

Complicating the simple idea of the pure and innocent child are William Blake's ideas on the contraries of innocence and experience: the innocent child is also the oppressed child, and the oppressed child learns to survive by turning the tables on his or her oppressor. In other words, for every Oliver Twist generated by society, we also get an Artful Dodger. In children's literature, this almost Manichean duality of children is best evident in George MacDonald's late fairy tale, *The Lost Princess* (1875), in which Agnes and Rosamund, the two main child characters, are complete opposites—the one tractable and capable of betterment, and the other intractable and incapable of betterment.

By century's end an attitude toward children that amounted to a "cult" affects much literature and art that deals with children. The child is the innocent, the pure fount from which we come and to which we wish to return. John Everett Millais's famous painting, *Bubbles* (1886), or J. M. Barrie's *Peter Pan* (1905), or Burnett's own *Little Lord Fauntleroy* (1886) illustrate this yearning for the beauty and innocence of childhood. In the child might be found the values associated with pastoral, with an England that was fast receding into the past with the advent of the railway, the motorcar, and the steamship. In the modern urban wasteland where adults must work in a hurried manner and in unpleasant places, the child represents some hope for escape from drudgery and some evidence of a kinder and gentler existence.

A Little Princess chronicles the growth of a child from seven to early adolescence, and what Burnett wants to argue is that growth need not be synonymous with decline, with the fall from innocence into a jaded experience, even if the child experiences hardship and deprivation. At the outset of the novel, Sara is clearly the pampered beautiful child of such evocations of the child cult as *Bubbles* or Mary Molesworth's *Hermy: The Story of a Little Girl.* She is wise beyond her years ("She felt as if she had lived a long, long time" [7]), yet she clings to her father when she thinks how strange it is to be one day living in India and not long after to be "in the middle of the ocean," and then to drive through a place "where the day was as dark as the night" (7). In other words, Burnett wants her reader to accept an anomaly: a child who is at once both wise and independent and puzzled and dependent.

As a child, Sara represents instinctive goodness. When she is nine she meets Becky, the scullery maid, who is 14, and she immediately feels kindly toward her. As the book goes on, Sara befriends not only

Becky but also the younger girl Lottie and the slow-witted Ermengarde. Even after she falls into disgrace with Miss Minchin, Sara remains the center of affection for many of the other children: "Her small pupils loved her, and strove with each other for the privilege of standing close to her and insinuating their small hands into hers" (115). By the end of the novel, Sara has not relinquished this attraction she holds for other children and adults: the Carmichaels had never "dreamed of such delights as resulted from an intimate acquaintance with the little-girl-who-was-not-a-beggar" (218). For this family, Sara has become a "priceless possession" (218). Sara remains a center of attention telling and retelling her story to members of the Large Family and to Mr. Carrisford.

Burnett does not take Sara into adulthood, but the fact that Sara continues, after her removal to Mr. Carrisford's house, to tell stories suggests that her future as a storyteller is secure. Also, her desire to feed the populace suggests that her sympathy for others has not diminished. Sara will take the powers of childhood into adulthood, and consequently she stands as a model for the young reader to emulate and for the older reader to admire. As is the case with many books for young readers, *A Little Princess* articulates a vision of childhood that is restorative; the child not only provides a model of behavior, but she is also a symbol of health and hope. The relationship between Sara and Mr. Carrisford, in other words, owes something to that between Eppie and Silas Marner in George Eliot's novel (1861). The adult may be able to bring material comfort to the child, but the child brings spiritual comfort to the adult.

6

Images of Sara, Images of Empire: Covers and Illustrations

Here I want to look at the primary experience of the visual even within the literary experience. Every book offers the reader something to look at even before he or she begins to read the opening page, and books for young readers clearly illustrate this. Versions of Sara Crewe's story are nearly all illustrated, and I propose to look at the beginning of the narrative in several of its manifestations—the first book form, the later novel, and more recent paperback editions—to illustrate the primacy of the visual in this literary experience. Despite our focus on the printed word, our initial experience of a text is visual. This is perhaps most apparent in books for young readers, where convention dictates that the written word be accompanied by illustration. But all of us first look at a book before we begin to read it; contrary to popular belief, we do judge, or at least begin to judge, a book by its cover. The cover offers us our first peek at what's underneath.

Take, for instance, the cover of *Sara Crewe; or, What Happened at Miss Minchin's.* My hardcover copy is an 1892 reprint that reproduces the cover design of the first edition. The flower pattern and military, or at least ceremonial, banner bring together female and male

Cover of *Sara Crewe; or, What Happened at Miss Minchin's,* by Frances Hodgson Burnett (New York: Charles Scribner's Sons, 1892).

images. This is a book which seeks readers of both sexes. This might account for the somewhat androgynous look of the figure—presumably Sara—in the golden circle within the medallion or shield at the left end of the banner. Sara sits contemplatively with a book suspended from her hand. Her position on the chair is back to front; she does not sit in the normal fashion. Here is an intelligent and unconventional young person. She stares at the fireplace in which a kettle rests. Balancing the book in the lower third of the picture is a fire iron. The fire motif repeats at the top and bottom of the circle that encloses Sara, not breaking the circle's dark line but suggesting nonetheless the possibility of eruption. Female/male, enclosure/eruption, book/iron, flower/banner: such binaries structure what we see and suggest interpretive possibilities even before we begin to read. At the very least, the design on the cover reaches out to a certain readership, to readers who will not care that the words of the title must appear on both sides of the banner. The twists in the banner might tell us that reading is not as linear a process as we might think. One more observation: the suggestion of things military that might seem so out of place in a book that apparently has nothing to do with the military (Sara's father's military career receives only passing mention) is an important sign of England's imperial enterprise, which forms the backdrop to the story.

A more recent reprint of *Sara Crewe* by Scholastic (1963), illustrated by Brian Wildsmith, has a colorful flower pattern reminiscent of late-nineteenth-century wallpaper for its cover design. The edges of the design are clipped in black, perhaps forewarning the reader of Sara's mourning for her father. But the flower pattern is bright, warm, and Victorian. When we turn to the cover of the longer *A Little Princess,* the hints we picked up from the cover of *Sara Crewe* speak more loudly. Sara is now bound by a series of rectangles formed most obviously by the picture frame and then the motifs of flower and staff that appear more open at the top than at the bottom. The picture shows a girl kneeling before a straight-back wooden chair, on which sits a doll. Behind the chair is a folding screen with what appears to be a flower design. Behind the girl and to her left is a table draped with a pink cloth. On the table sits a large pot with a green plant. Above and behind the plant we see a picture on the wall, and on the floor is a carpet. I mention these details because nothing here directly suggests the poverty and drudgery of Sara's life, which forms the plot of the novel. We might say the same of what we see on the covers of the two editions of *Sara Crewe* I mentioned earlier. In fact, the picture with the title of the book (the title sits above the picture and its

Cover of *A Little Princess,* by Frances Hodgson Burnett (London: Frederick Warne & Co., n.d.).

decorative border) forming a straight and formal upper border to the design depicts little but a young girl apparently speaking and gesturing to a doll. This is the first indication of the importance of the doll in the story; the doll is an integral part of the visual introduction to the story in all its forms.

An exception to these covers is the one for the Puffin paperback edition published in 1961 and reprinted regularly at least until 1973. Here the drudgery of Sara's life is evident in the charcoal colored dress she wears, her unkempt hair, the bareness of the room and floor on which she sits, and the rat in the foreground. Not evident here is the martial or imperial theme. In contrast, the cover of the 1990 Signet edition draws attention to Victorian pertness in the main character. It sports a reproduction of William Jabez Muckley's painting *Youthful Vanity*, apparently wanting to draw attention to the self-reflexive aspects of the main character. The idea of "vanity" as it reflects on Sara is intriguing—an interpretation that would side with Lavinia and perhaps reflect a modern slant on Burnett's early Edwardian female hero. Sara's readiness to consider herself a princess is, at best, cute, childish vanity.

The early covers, then, do not stress the hardship Sara endures during the action of the story. They do, however, signal the imperial theme. I mentioned this earlier in noticing the military banner on *Sara Crewe*'s cover; the cover of *A Little Princess* is, perhaps, less direct. The carpet, the pot, and the plant suggest to me the late nineteenth century's interest in things exotic. They are redolent of the tropics, the far-flung Empire and what it can offer the mother country. They are offerings to Sara, signs of obeisance to the little princess. The covers of these books reflect what Edward Said calls the "illusion of benevolence" (Said, xvii), and they, as well as the story itself, call for what he terms a "contrapuntal reading"—that is, a reading "able to think through and interpret together experiences that are discrepant, each with its particular agenda and pace of development, its own internal formations, its internal coherence and system of external relationships, all of them co-existing and interacting with others" (Said, 32). In the case of Burnett's book, we have an acceptance, virtually without consciousness, of the rightness of Empire, while in India itself the movement for independence was growing. The covers of these editions can remind us that England's Empire is as important to an understanding of *A Little Princess* as any other context we might wish to develop, formal or thematic.

Another aspect of these covers is their consciousness of space. Sara is shown within a clearly defined space: the circle on the cover of

Sara Crewe and the rectangle on that of *A Little Princess.* It's as if we are peeking at the little girl through a window, a doorway, or a lens; we are voyeurs seeing the girl in her rightful place—in the home, and in one instance near the hearth. At the very least, we are spectators seeing a moment of the story's action stilled within the framing circle or rectangle. What is hidden, screened as it were, from our view is the careful constructing of a female suitable for the male gaze. In terms of the books' plots, Sara is the object of the voyeuristic peeking of Ram Dass, who, acting on the directions of his master, Mr. Carrisford, reinscribes the orphaned Sara as the little princess who will care for her new male benefactor. In other words, the circumscribing or enclosing of the girl within circle and rectangle begins to construct, literally to place, her. She belongs in a domestic setting. Daughters of the Empire have a duty to bring affection and care to their men; Sara's one desire, we learn in *A Little Princess,* is to "keep house for her father; to ride with him and to sit at the head of his table when he had dinner-parties; to talk to him and read his books" (9). At the end of the book she achieves something of this desire when she makes her home with her surrogate father, Mr. Carrisford.

One might argue that no one examines the cover of a book as deliberately as I have just done. Perhaps not. But the point is that our first experience of a book must be its cover and what we see begins to affect how we think, even unconsciously, about the book. Readers of the Puffin paperback I have described receive no signal of the imperial theme from the cover. Instead, it stresses relationships, both Sara's relationship with Melchisedec, the rat, and with another girl, perhaps Becky. Published in the 1960s, this edition picks up the decade's interest in natural relationships. From another perspective, the glum looks on both girls' faces, their sacklike dresses, and the short hair of one might remind some of the civilians rounded up in Nazi concentration camps. However we view this cover, our interpretation of the book (of any book) receives a nudge in a certain direction by what we see on the cover. The visual is primary.

As a reader turns the first leaves of the early editions of *Sara Crewe* and *A Little Princess* she encounters a frontispiece, a visual introduction to the story. The frontispiece in both books contrasts what we have already seen on the covers. In Reginald Birch's frontispiece in *Sara Crewe* (Birch collaborated several times with Burnett) we see Sara in the center of the composition, seated on a footstool and bent over her doll in what the rest of the picture prompts us to interpret as a mood of sadness. We view the scene from within the room: bare walls poorly plastered, slanting ceiling with wooden beams framing a skylight, fireplace, lighted candle, broken pitcher, broom handle, trunk, assorted glass bottles, partly opened hat-box, string suspended from slanting ceiling to wall. There are no chairs or comfortable seating, no bed, no carpet on the floor. Sara sits directly under the skylight. The whole composition is richly suggestive, especially in light of the words printed below the picture: "She laid her doll, Emily, across her knees, and put her face down upon her, and her arms around her, and sat there, not saying one word, not making one sound." The words interpret, or interfere with, our visual experience of the page. They purport to offer an explanation of the picture, but what actually happens is that the picture explains the words. The words merely describe what Sara does: she puts her head over her doll that lies on her knees, embraces the doll, and remains silent. The added information in the illustration might prompt us to interpret Sara's mood as sad. She might be grieving. Of course, she might simply be in a contemplative mood, but too much depends on what we see. The skylight, placed strategically above Sara, throws its light against the wall behind and also over her. What does this signify? Does the picture offer hope that something good will shine on Sara from above, or does it reinforce through the high leaded window Sara's imprisonment, her life of drudgery? What can have happened at Miss Minchin's to have produced this contemplative or this grief-laden moment? The illustration, then, functions to draw the reader in, to place her inside the story, yet leaves her unable to know what has happened until she reads further.

Harold Piffard's frontispiece to *A Little Princess* works in a dissimilar manner but to the same end: to draw the reader into the story. Here we have a color illustration showing Sara and Ram Dass; in other words, this illustration emphasizes the book's imperial theme. Ram Dass stands behind a table set with a lace-bordered white cloth, blue

"She laid her doll, Emily, across her knees, and put her face down upon her, and her arms around her, and sat there, not saying one word, not making one sound." Frontispiece illustration by Reginald Birch, *Sara Crewe; or, What Happened at Miss Minchin's,* by Frances Hodgson Burnett (New York: Charles Scribner's Sons, 1892).

china, food, and a lighted lamp. Sara stands to the left of the table, one hand on it and the other on a chair. Behind her is a screen, reminding us of the screen visible on the cover illustration. On the wall, top right, hangs a picture, and stuck behind it is what appears to be a fan. The picture is difficult to decipher, but visible are two characters, one of which is dressed in a red cape and hood. The shadow of Ram Dass looms on the wall between him and Sara. Below the illustration is the caption "Ram Dass was standing smiling into her startled face." The give and take of verbal and visual is as nicely set out as we could wish for. The reader who sees this picture before knowing the story must find the smiling Ram Dass somewhat ambivalent because the illustration presents him as a dark figure. I use "dark" here precisely because it is loaded. Ram Dass's shadow, tilted as it is over Sara, gives the illustration a threatening look. The smile, to those of us who know the story, is sincere and benign, but to the innocent reader it might just as easily be sinister. Certainly, the look on Sara's face registers suspicion.

And let's stop for a moment on the picture hanging behind Ram Dass. Might the red-clad figure be Red Riding Hood? A reading of the book gives us no direct (or even indirect, I think) allusion to the story of the little girl and the wolf. But without having read Burnett's novel, the innocent reader might just apply the Red Riding Hood story to what she or he sees here. Who, then, is the wolf? And can we sustain a reading of the story through this trope of Red Riding Hood? My guess is that we can, assuming that Sara is the girl apparently threatened by England's Asian colony, but ultimately saved by a son of Empire, the so-called Indian gentleman who is, in fact, Mr. Carrisford, Englishman par excellance. However we read this illustration, either as a sign of the "darkness" of the colonies or as a sign of the bounty the colonies offer (fan, food, china, servant), one thing is certain: to look at it is to see clearly the importance to this book of England's imperial activities.

More recent editions of the story, in their illustrations, show a slightly more sensitive approach to the issue of Empire. Brian Wildsmith's illustrations to *Sara Crewe* offer only one look at Ram Dass, and this is a distance view in which Ram Dass is present with Mr. Carrisford and Sara. The swirl of Sara's hairdo looks similar to Ram Dass's turban, effectively negating the turban as a sign of "other-

"Ram Dass was standing smiling into her startled face." Frontispiece illustration by Harold Piffard, *A Little Princess,* by Frances Hodgson Burnett (London: Frederick Warne & Co., n.d.).

ness." Ram Dass's clothing is a sign of his origins, but this, too, is not strongly presented to the reader. In short, this edition tries to soften the book's approach to Empire. As another indication of this, note that Sara calls the monkey a "queer, poor, ugly, strange little thing" (73). The early editions of the story do not have the word *strange* here; instead, you will read the word *foreign*.

The Puffin edition has illustrations by Margery Gill. Of the 24 illustrations, only one shows Ram Dass, and once again we see him only from a distance. Nowhere in evidence are uniforms or other military paraphernalia. The focus in these illustrations is on Sara, her friends, and their enclosed world. More often than not Gill pictures Sara with Ermengarde or Becky, and the number of persons in the pictures increases as we near the end of the book. The emphasis is on relationships and the importance of friendship. This edition dates from the early 1960s, and its concern is with Sara's growing up. Perhaps this edition's sensitivity to cultural matters is, once again, best noticed in the alteration of a word. In chapter 10 of the early editions, Lottie speaks of the new neighbor as a "yellow gentleman," and she asks Sara whether she thinks this man "is a Chinee" because her geography book "says the Chinee men are yellow." The Puffin edition changes the word *Chinee* to the less disagreeable *Chinese* (121).

My own response rues such changes in language and illustrations that mute the imperial theme, and I note in passing that the Signet edition restores the original *Chinee. A Little Princess* depends for its plot on the fact of Empire; without colonial India, Sara's father would stay with her and possibly even have longevity; without colonial India, Mr. Carrisford would not have an Indian servant who can slip across the roofs of London's row housing to bring magic to Sara; without England's colonies, the monkey would not have appeared to bring Sara into contact with Ram Dass. But such plot devices are of less importance than the casualness with which Burnett uses the Empire, her complete lack of awareness that she appropriates another culture and people for her own purposes. Readers today deserve to know this, not to be protected from such knowledge.

7

The Importance of Empire: Stage Version and Film Adaptations

A look at Burnett's script of her play *The Little Princess* shows just how conscious she was—and how conscious she wants her audience to be—of visual objects. First we read a list of the properties, an extensive list numbering 56 items. Then we have instructions for setting the scene, for the lighting at curtain's rise, and for the position of the players. The instructions for the scene are explicit, even numbering the bracket-lamps and the maps on the wall, and stipulating the color of the carpet. The action is bound—bound by the proscenium arch, by the schoolroom with its prominent window center stage, by the very weather visible out the window. Before the actors begin to speak, the audience sees a cozy warm room with children dancing and singing. We also see two children, one of them is Lavinia, off to the right, outside the group of dancing children. This shows us the odd ones out in this community of girls.

Whereas both prose versions of the story begin outside Miss Minchin's and announce the sense of enclosure either through repetition of words and sounds or by situating the action inside a cab, the play version can—and must—begin within a clearly defined space. To put this another way, we know that a narrated story allows for the narrator to provide information in words that a drama provides visually. The space in which the narrative will take place is immediately evident in the drama, although in the novel the narrator might move the narrated events easily through several different spaces. The filming of stage plays often "opens up" the sense of space in this way. The same is true of time. The narrator of a novel might move from one moment to another without elaborate preparation; Burnett, for example, is fond of shifts into the past (flashbacks) in her prose fiction. On the other hand, all versions of a narrative may use such devices as shifts into the past and future to communicate information to an audience either through information passed on by a narrator or by the actors in a drama. Here we move to the importance of the word and away from the visual, although in film flashbacks or flashforwards might appear visually; the pantomine or dumbshow on stage might accomplish the same thing.

It is true that both the first version of this story, *Sara Crewe; or What Happened at Miss Minchin's,* and the stage play mute the theme of Empire. Little is made of the Indian connection directly in these versions, although I note two moments, one in each version, as indicators that we ought not to neglect Empire and its significance. At one point in *Sara Crewe,* little Sara thinks that perhaps the Indian gentleman's servant, whom she calls a Lascar, "saved his master's life in the Sepoy rebellion" (*Sara,* 68). She refers here to what is commonly known as "the Great Mutiny" that occurred in 1857. Edward Said notes that Indian historians refer to this event as a "Rebellion," whereas British historians refer to it as a "Mutiny" (Said, 146). Its mention in passing in *Sara Crewe* illustrates just how deeply the sense of a rebellion quashed entered the British psyche. Sara presumes that the Indian servant saved the life of his colonial master during that "rebellion/mutiny" that stands for the people of India as a major event in their desire for independence from colonial masters. The 1905 novel excises this passage for plot reasons rather than for ideological ones; in *Sara Crewe* Sara's father is much younger than Mr. Carrisford, but in *A Little Princess* the two men are friends of about the same age.

The stage play, as we might expect, uses a visual means of reminding the audience of Empire. Of course, Ram Dass appears on stage and speaks in a conventional "native servant" manner. And Sara reports to Ermengarde how Ram Dass "salaams to me when he sees me" (*Play,* 40). More telling, however, are the stage directions to act 3. This act takes place in Mr. Carrisford's study, and among the stage directions we have this: "Oriental rugs on floor with a tiger's-head rug c. down stage for Donald" (*Play,* 54). Donald is one of Mr. Charmichael's children; earlier in the play he had, according to the stage directions, received Lottie's offer of Sara's doll by boxing "it away from him, boy fashion" (*Play,* 21). In act 3 he will once again act in "boy fashion" by making a nuisance of himself in one way and another; at one point he rides the tiger's-head rug "boisterously" (*Play,* 55). Later he makes it clear that Sara's father shot this particular tiger, and then the act ends with him standing on the tiger's head. This image—virtually an icon—of the boy standing on the tiger's-head is surely an image of England's destiny; the boy is the conquering hero standing on the symbol of those far-flung places now dominated by British forces.

I seem to have shifted my attention from the primacy of the visual to the importance of Empire for an understanding of Burnett's story. Actually, the two are difficult to disentangle because, as I have tried to show, what we see are images and signs of Empire. Just as Burnett finds it easy to place her story on the imperial stage because she writes at the imperial moment, so, too, is the story easy to adapt for less subtle, even jingoistic, support of Empire. What I look to here is the 1939 film of the story—a film that announces that it derives from Burnett's novel. The film stars Shirley Temple and is directed by Walter Lang (this was in fact the second film version of the story, the first being the 1917 silent film starring Mary Pickford). The screenplay appears to derive in some measure from the stage version, and it also departs from all previous versions in several ways. The point here, however, is the primacy of the visual and its focus on the imperial theme.

The film begins with the words "England 1899" superimposed on the British coat of arms. The following shots are a montage of images of Empire—Tower Bridge, the Tower of London, Windsor Castle, British soldier in bearskin hat, marching troops, a newspaper announcing battle in South Africa, and a portrait of the queen, that quintessential icon of Empire, Victoria. While we watch these images we hear the strains of "Rule Britannia" on the soundtrack. Cut to the interior of a horse-drawn cab where a child and a male adult speak about the Boers "misbehaving" in South Africa. The child—Shirley Temple as Sara Crewe—wears clothes that echo those of royalty. Her ermine ruff and stoll reflect her status as the "little princess" and foreshadow the appearance of Queen Victoria late in the film. As we get to know the characters, much is made of little Sara behaving like a good soldier. Her upper lip is stiff and she marches, salutes, and talks as a soldier should. The film, of course, reflects the realities of the late 1930s, when it was made. On the brink of a European war, Hollywood offers a grand vision of British imperial glory, where even the children are good little soldiers. Much of the last third of the film takes place inside a military hospital, a location completely absent from any of Burnett's versions.

Fifty-six years later Hollywood returns to this story for the 1995 film *A Little Princess,* directed by Alfonso Cuaron. The film is one of several retelling classic children's stories to appear in recent years: for example, Rudyard Kipling's *The Jungle Book* (1995), George MacDonald's *The Princess and the Goblin* (1991), L. M. Montgomery's *Anne of Green Gables* (1985), Hans Christian Andersen's *The Little Mermaid* (1989) and *Thumbelina* (1994), Louisa May Alcott's *Little Women* (1995), Anna Sewell's *Black Beauty* (1994), Marjorie Rawlings's *The Yearling* (1994), and Burnett's *The Secret Garden* (1993). The story of Sara Crewe seems tailor-made for our cultural moment, focusing as it does on questions of economic hardship, success through perseverance and individual initiative, and intercultural relationships.

Rather than go to school in England, Sara (played by Liesel Matthews) goes to school in New York in 1914. Her father is going off to fight in World War I, and he leaves Sara at Miss Minchin's school because this is the same school Sara's mother attended. The film takes its cue from the 1939 film in which Captain Crewe goes to fight the Boers in South Africa. War stands in for the mining activities in India that occur in Burnett's story. It is clear why the 1939 film chooses to locate the action against the backdrop of war, and it is interesting to speculate that the 1995 film does something similar for similar reasons.

I refer, of course, to the period of unrest in the 1990s that has seen the Gulf War, the tensions in the Middle East, the civil war in the former Yugoslavia, and terrorist activity even on the Northern American continent. The impact of war—or at least of acts of military or paramilitary violence—strikes nearly all of us. The film might well be a reminder of just how vulnerable even the most innocent are to the sorrows brought by war.

Another aspect of the film is its handling of the imperial theme. Despite the fact that the action takes place in New York and in the battlefields of Europe, the story does include Ram Dass and references to India. Ram Dass is the inscrutable "other": he has almost no dialogue in the film but his presence always reminds us of what the opening of the film refers to as the "mystical land" of India. Sara's father remarks early in the film, "India's the only place on earth that stirs the imagination." Even more than in earlier versions, India here is less a real place than the site of desire. It represents a fantasy of fulfilled desire, and as such it serves as a backdrop to the story of Sara and her tribulations. Throughout the film we have glimpses of Sara's fantasy life—snippets of a story from the *Ramayana* concerning Prince Rama and Princess Sita. Sara perceives these fantasy characters as her father (Liam Cunningham plays both Captain Crewe and Prince Rama) and mother (Princess Sita is played by Alison Moir, and photographs we see in Sara's locket and on the walls at Miss Minchin's Seminary make it clear that she is also Sara's mother). In other words, Sara does not in any real sense accept this story as expressive of another country and culture: she uses it for her own gratification, effectively claiming the story for her own imaginary purposes. At the end of the film, Sara, her father, and Becky leave for "home," which we must assume is India. As the film recedes into an iris, we can conclude that home/India is a fantasy land, a place of the imagination, rather than the India into which Gandhi is emerging.

It is worth noting that the film offers itself as sensitive to racial matters; having the characters from the *Ramayana* be Sara's mother and father illustrates that Sara does not fear the "other," that she is not consciously prejudiced. That the story reflects on her Oedipal fantasies (she desires her father with an intensity that borders on the indiscreet), however, only reinforces how the film removes the *Ramayana* from its cultural context. In short, the use of India by the filmmakers perpetuates an imperial attitude to that country. Color is also an issue here, as Prince Rama in Sara's fantasy is blue, distancing him completely from actual humanity. Having characters from an Indian myth played by Caucasian actors might signify the psychological nature of Sara's fantasizing, but it also perpetuates a type of cultural appropriation Hollywood has practiced for years. (In the 1939, for example, Ram Dass is played by Cesar Romero, and in countless period films North America's native peoples have been portrayed by white actors.)

Something similar might be said about the film's use of the American locale. Set in New York in 1914, the film deals with a private school for girls, and, as we might expect, it is a school for white girls only. In the original version, England's class system comes under scrutiny partly in the character of Becky, the scullery maid. In this film version Becky is black. One of the schoolgirls, Lottie, explains to Sara that the students do not speak with Becky because she is a "servant girl" and she has "dark skin." When Sara remarks, "So What?" Lottie replies, "Doesn't that mean something?" And of course it does mean something. The unspoken message is that black children are not among the privileged; education is closed to them. So far, this historical peek at the social injustice perpetrated on a minority is salutary. The film goes on, however, to perpetuate the stereotype of the black person as an appendage to the white "master." Becky remains Sara's servant, someone under the influence of Sara. What comes to mind here is the recent Newbery Medal winner *Maniac Magee* (1990), by Jerry Spinelli. Both the film and Spinelli's book offer a rather glib liberal humanist version of race relations in which the white person stands out as sensitive, intelligent, and caring and the black person is meek, diffident, and appreciative. The white person serves as mentor and even guardian to the black person. Burnett's story may have served a radical purpose in its day, but from the perspective of the 1990s, it does little to interrogate a continuing drive for white supremacy. And the new film version simply perpetuates Burnett's unconscious championing of a white middle class.

8

Emily: A Living Doll

In the brief preface to *Racketty-Packetty House,* a short story for children that Burnett published in 1906, "Queen Crosspatch," who supposedly authors this story, writes, "If you think dolls never do anything you don't see them do, you are very much mistaken. When people are not looking at them they can do anything they choose. They can dance and sing and play on the piano and have all sorts of fun. But they can only move about and talk when people turn their backs and are not looking."[30] Sara Crewe testifies to a similar attitude to dolls when she first takes Ermengarde to her rooms. She warns Ermengarde to go quietly so that they might catch her doll, Emily, walking about the room. When Ermengarde expresses incredulity, Sara explains that she believes Emily can walk about, or at least "I *pretend* I believe she can. And that makes it seem as if it were true" (31). Earlier she had told her French maid, Mariette, that she believes "Emily can read and walk and talk, but she will only do it when people are out of the room. That is her secret" (20).

Truth and reality are what we believe they are. We here touch on Burnett's theme of magic, that ingredient in life that infuses the world with wonder. If we believe, then what we believe is true. Build it and they will come. Believe the attic room in Miss Minchin's is a beautiful suite and it will be so. What appears lifeless and inanimate is, if we think it is, full of life. This urging for us to believe in the possibility of fantastic things going on in the world just outside our sight is a familiar theme at the turn of the century; we can find it in Conan Doyle's belief in fairies, in the spiritualism of Madame Blavatsky, in James Barrie's *Peter Pan,* in E. Nesbit's Psammead stories, and even in some of H. G. Wells's writing. In the case of Burnett, this belief in a sort of fairy realm is a logical extension of the romantic ethos as it evolved in the nineteenth century. The early century was taken with the wonders of galvanism, mesmerism, and animal magnetism; one result of this interest was the appearance in literature of automata, animated statues, doppelgängers, and the like. If mind and matter are fundamentally alike, then inanimate matter could be brought to life. Perhaps inanimate matter actually manifested the life force despite appearances to the contrary.

The early century's interest in science, which resulted in such works as Mary Shelley's *Frankenstein* (1818), becomes in the Victorian period touched with a Christian sensibility, as such works as George MacDonald's *Phantastes* (1858) or *David Elginbrod* (1864) or Bulwer Lytton's *A Strange Story* (1862) illustrate. Although this belief in another realm interconnecting with the one we perceive has many sources, MacDonald and Lytton were well read in German literature and philosophy of the late-eighteenth and early-nineteenth centuries. That Burnett knew this work, too, is evident from her late novel, *The Land of the Blue Flower* (1908), in which the longing for a better world, the world associated with the German writer Novalis's blue flower, is readily apparent. In *A Little Princess* Burnett expresses this longing for a better world in her notion of "magic." The magic that transforms Sara's dreary life can transform all life if only we give it a chance, if only we believe in it. The belief that a doll is alive is "beautiful" (31), Sara tells Ermengarde, and we later see that to believe in another state of affairs than the one we experience is also beautiful.

Of course, Sara's doll also serves a rather less rarified purpose in the novel and in Sara's life. Emily comforts Sara. At the beginning of the book Sara and her father go shopping for a special doll, one that will be Sara's friend once her father leaves for India: "I want her to talk to about him" (13). Sara tells Miss Minchin that "Emily is going to be my intimate friend" (13). But Emily is more than a friend, more than a reminder of Captain Crewe when he is away from his daughter; she also a sign of Sara's desperate need for a companion and a mother. Sara has enjoyed a life of comfort in material things, but she has never known her mother and has had no other children to play with. Her father has been her constant companion, and as he prepares to leave her, he can only think that she "ought to play more with dolls" (13), not that she ought to play with girls her own age.

Sara takes Emily, then, as her companion. She looks upon the doll as a person, one who deserves fine clothes. She and her father take Emily to "a children's outfitter's shop" where Emily was "measured for a wardrobe as grand as Sara's own. She had lace frocks, too, and velvet and muslin ones, and hats and coats and beautiful lace-trimmed underclothes, and gloves and handkerchiefs and furs" (16). Sara accepts the rightness of finery. She also assumes the role of Emily's mother: "I'm her mother, though I am going to make a companion of her" (16). This assumption of the mother's role reflects both Sara's nurturing instinct (she also serves as Lottie's mother) and her longing for a mother. It is, perhaps, no accident that Sara and her father buy Emily after they have met Miss Minchin, for Miss Minchin proves unsuitable, even on a first meeting, to be Sara's surrogate mother. Left by herself in a strange environment, Sara needs the comfort of a mother, and her only resource is a doll.

Whether we perceive her as Sara's child, her companion, or her mother, Emily fulfills an important role in Sara's introduction to the pupils at Miss Minchin's academy. The doll serves as a point of contact between Ermengarde and Sara, and between the younger children and Sara; the children regard Sara "as a goddess and a queen" after they share tea with Sara and her doll (37). For these children, Emily is a sign of Sara's favored position in the school and in life; she represents wealth. Even more a sign of luxury is the "Last Doll" that arrives for Sara's eleventh birthday. This doll wears a cloak lined with ermine and carries an opera-glass in her hand. She also has a trunk filled with lace collars and silk stockings, a jewel-case "containing a necklace and a tiara which looked quite as if they were made of real diamonds," hats and tea-gowns and fans (70).

But Sara's wealth appears to evaporate on the news of her father's death. She must give up her favored status in the school and remove to the attic. She clings to Emily as her only comfort, and as a reminder of happier times with her father. With her change in status, however, Sara begins to change in other ways; she begins to mature. With no other companion in her dreary attic room, Sara begins to contemplate Emily, and a "strange feeling" about Emily comes to her (115). She tries to maintain the fiction that Emily can think and feel, and from this fiction she even begins to take a lesson. Because Emily remains unresponsive to Sara's questions, Sara thinks this is a strategy, aimed at preserving one's sense of power and worth in the face of insult and mistreatment. She recalls how, when she herself remains reticent in the face of Miss Minchin's or the other girls' insults, they become angry or even frightened: "When you will not fly into a passion people know you are stronger than they are, because you are strong enough to hold in your rage, and they are not, and they say stupid things they wish they hadn't said afterward. There's nothing so strong as rage, except what makes you hold it in—that's stronger" (116).

As useful as such lessons might be, they do not overcome the feelings of desolation Sara feels when her employers work her long hours and treat her unkindly. One day she returns to her attic room particularly tired and hungry, "with a tempest raging in her young breast" (116). She pours her heart out to Emily, but the doll sits impassively, as usual. Suddenly, Sara loses her temper:

> She looked at the staring glass eyes and complacent face, and suddenly a sort of heartbroken rage seized her. She lifted her little savage hand and knocked Emily off the chair, bursting into a passion of sobbing—Sara who never cried. "You are nothing but a *doll;*" she cried; "nothing but a doll—doll—doll! You care for nothing. You are stuffed with sawdust. You never had a heart. Nothing could ever make you feel. You are a *doll*!" (117)

The emphasis on the word *doll* tells us how strong Sara's rejection of childish fancy is; she is about to put away childish things. Her tears are also a sign of maturity. Sara has up to now refused to cry, and her lack of tears revealed how unnatural this child was. What comes to mind is George MacDonald's story "The Light Princess" (1864), in which the princess is unnaturally gay, never experiencing sorrow and never crying. Only with the advent of tears does she show maturity and the accompanying ability to feel sympathy for others. Similarly, once Sara regains her composure she thinks of others, if not with compassion then certainly with understanding. She tells Emily that she "can't help being a doll . . . any more than Lavinia and Jesse can help not having any sense. We are not all made alike" (117).

Before we leave this passage, we might note one thing more: the word *savage*. By knocking Emily off the chair, Sara acts like a savage. The word is redolent of Empire, a theme we looked at earlier. The natives of the far-flung colonies are invariably marked by the word *savage*. The street waif, Anne, to whom Sara gives hot baked buns later in the story, is likewise a "savage." In fact, on the final page of the book we learn that Anne is "no longer a savage" (301). The message here is that good English girls can, through deprivation, neglect, unkindness, and poverty, sink to the level of a "savage." The savage is only good for the work of drudgery. Unlike so many Victorian stories that show adversity and illness as necessary moral agents of renovation, *A Little Princess* shows how one good, if spoiled, little girl, might be in danger of reduction to the state of savagery. Again, it is no accident that directly after this incident in which Sara shows her "savage" side, the Indian gentleman moves in next door and Sara's recovery begins. It is also no accident that Emily's part in the story is nearly over.

9

Books, Stories, and Power

The doll, Emily, is a comfort to Sara, reminding her of her father and conjuring up, if unconsciously, the image of the mother. She also serves to remind us of the importance of play to a child. When Captain Crewe tells Miss Minchin early in the novel that Sara ought to play with dolls more than she does, his reasoning is that she reads too much. He tells the schoolmistress that Sara "is always sitting with her little nose burrowing into books. She doesn't read them, Miss Minchin; she gobbles them up as if she were a little wolf instead of a little girl. She is always starving for new books to gobble, and she wants grown-up books—great, big, fat ones—French and German as well as English—history and biography and poets, and all sorts of things" (13). Clearly, reading also serves a need for this young girl; she derives comfort from books, just as she derives it from her doll. One of the most impressive moments in the novel comes when Sara asks Ermengarde to lend her the books Ermengarde's father sends. When Ermengarde responds by saying she will give Sara anything, Sara replies, "I don't want you to give me anything. . . . I want your books—I want them!" And "her eyes grew big, and her chest heaved" (160). Sara's desire for books is physical. Both books and doll provide impetus to Sara's imaginative life.

Burnett is on unsure ground here. First, we learn that Sara reads too much, that she ought to play more often with dolls or go riding her pony. The trace here is to Rousseauistic and Wordsworthian notions of healthy play. Just as the children in *The Secret Garden* receive health and mental vigor from their outside activities, Sara, too, would do well to get healthy exercise. Yet her reading proves a life line during her time of hardship. Because she has read so much, she has material with which to exercise her imagination, and she can pretend that her attic room is the Bastille and that she and Becky are prisoners. Just as princesses during the French Revolution found themselves imprisoned and hounded by the unpleasant rabble, so, too, was Sara a princess unjustly incarcerated in her attic room. Sara's sympathy for the likes of the Princesse de Lamballe sits easily with her sympathy for the populace. In other words, her reading has resulted in a naive ability to side with both the oppressors and the oppressed.

Sara reads a variety of books—"all sorts of things"—but she reads everything as if it was fiction. Indeed, she approaches the world as if it were one grand narrative. She tells Ermengarde, "*Everything's* a story. You are a story—I am a story. Miss Minchin is a story" (109). For Sara, *story* is another word for *romance,* although she never uses the word. By turning everything into romance, Sara can escape her mundane and dreary surroundings. But, as I said, Burnett is not certain of her theme here. Turning everything into romance allows Sara to survive her fall from grace; more important, it gives her power. This is evident even before her fall into poverty. Burnett's narrator, as usual, states the case bluntly:

> Of course the greatest power Sara possessed, and the one which gained her even more followers than her luxuries and the fact that she was "the show pupil," the power that Lavinia and certain other girls were most envious of, and at the same time most fascinated by in spite of themselves, was her power of telling stories and of making everything she talked about seem like a story, whether it was one or not. (44)

Sara is a natural storyteller. This power of speech is a communal one. Sara can create community with her story-telling. She also gains a sense of self-worth. The power to tell a story is the power, to a certain extent, to fashion the self and the self's world. Sara fancies herself a princess, and even when she experiences poverty she can maintain this sense of identity because of her ability to place herself inside her stories.

Sara's stories are, as I indicated, romances and fairy tales. Early in the novel, we see her captivating her schoolmates with a story about Mermaids and a Princess, reminiscent of Frances Browne's "Sour and Civil" (from *Granny's Wonderful Chair* [1856]) and Hans Christian Andersen's "The Little Mermaid." When Lavinia interrupts the storytelling to complain that the servant Becky is listening, Sara argues that anyone can listen because "stories belong to everybody" (47). An argument ensues in which Sara implies a connection between the Book of Revelation and fairy stories, suggesting that such stories have a truth value beyond the obvious. Sara asks Lavinia how she knows that her stories are fairy stories. Thus she appears to accept the popular notion of fairy stories as untrue, but in doing so she also raises the possibility that her stories are true in the way that the "much more splendid stories in Revelation" are true (47). The suggestion here is one repeated in Tolkien's famous essay "On Fairy Stories," in which he states that the best fairy story of all is to be found in the gospels. In other words, Sara touches on the notion of consolation that Tolkien argues—one of the most prominent aspects of fairy stories.

The question of the kind of truth offered by fairy stories is less straightforward than this. Recall the *Athenaeum* review that placed the theme of Empire in a fairy-tale context. Fairy tales and romances dress up the world; they are a form of wish fulfillment associated with dreams. Robert Louis Stevenson in *Treasure Island* (1878) calls romance "sea-dreams," and reality proves a far cry from these dreams of adventure that fill the innocent and youthful head of Jim Hawkins. In *A Little Princess* romance appears to be Sara's reality when she wakes to find her room transformed into a place of warmth and comfort. But the reader has, early in the novel, a warning about taking such waking dreams too seriously. At issue is the idea of storytelling. When Sara first meets Miss Minchin, she wonders why the schoolmistress calls her "a beautiful child." Thinking to herself that she is not beautiful, Sara concludes that Miss Minchin "is beginning by telling a story." She confesses that she, too, "should be telling a story" if she called Miss Minchin beautiful (12). Here the word *story* means falsehood; to tell a story is to lie. Thus before we ever learn of Sara's precocious talent for storytelling, we see the notion of story as dubious, false. And as the novel develops, we might see the force of Elizabeth Keyser's argument that Sara's growth has something to do with her acceptance of reality. By the end of the book, Sara's storytelling has evolved from fantasy to realism. She begins by telling a story about mermaids and a princess, then she adapts history to the form of story when she pretends to share the experiences of Marie Antoinette and the Princesse de Lamballe, and finally she tells the story of Anne, the street urchin she has seen and sympathized with.

Just as Sara's doll disappears, replaced by "a splendid boarhound," so, too, does Sara pass beyond the need for fairy tales. Perhaps one of the triumphs of the form of Burnett's novel is that it takes a fairy tale plot—that of "Cinderella," as many have noted—and folds it into a realistic context. Earlier writers for children such as Anne Ritchie and Harriet Childe-Pemberton had taken familiar fairy tales and recast them in contemporary realistic contexts, but Burnett in *Little Lord Fauntleroy, A Little Princess,* and *The Lost Prince* removes the reader from any direct allusion to fairy tales. In fact, we might say that the power of story in *A Little Princess* takes both Sara and the reader beyond story. By internalizing her sense of what a princess is from her reading of books, Sara turns to act in the real world by feeding the populace. The final gesture of the book is also an encouragement to the reader to go beyond the book and act in the reader's real world. Sara asks Anne to read the world the way that she, Sara, reads it; in the final paragraph the reader is in Anne's position, watching Sara and the Indian gentleman ride away in their carriage. Sara thinks Anne has understood her, but whether she has must remain a mystery, something only Anne knows. Whether the reader takes action from reading this book also remains a mystery, something only the reader knows.

10

Confinement: House and City

As much that I have said suggests, Sara's real world is not wide. Unlike male characters in children's books such as Jim Hawkins, Sara does not travel far for adventure. Her place is firmly domestic. The opening of the novel makes the point clearly: "Once on a dark winter's day, when the yellow fog hung so thick and heavy in the streets of London that the lamps were lighted and the shop windows blazed with gas as they do at night, an odd-looking little girl sat in a cab with her father, and was driven rather slowly through the big thorough-fares." The first six words are a neat inversion of the usual fairy-tale beginning: "once upon a time" becomes "once on a dark winter's day," a shrinking of the imaginatively expansive fairy-tale beginning to an almost equally general but more restricting focus on a particular day and season. In other words, the darkness, the season, and the thick fog introduce us to a closed world and prepare us for the restricted life of Sara at Miss Minchin's. Sara will be at the mercy of the elements and the spaces she inhabits, as she here is the passive passenger in a cab. The thoroughfares of London might be "big," but Sara's movement through them is controlled by the weather and the cab driver.

Although the narrator does not direct us to the cab window, we might acknowledge that Sara and her father can only look on the gas-lighted shop windows through the window of their cab. Windows are closely associated with Sara throughout the story. For example, Sara first talks with Ermengarde in a window seat; the two girls curl up in this seat and become friends. Significantly, outside they look upon a "dingy square" (29), a reminder of closed horizons. If a female is going to travel, she will do it in her head, imaginatively. Later, while Lottie and some of the young pupils play, Sara curls "herself up in the window-seat" and reads "a book about the French Revolution" (57). Later, once she has suffered demotion through poverty, Sara makes a habit of looking into people's houses through their windows, and she imagines all sorts of romantic things about what goes on in these houses. In short, Sara's life, like the life of nearly all women of her time, is severely circumscribed.

Once removed to the attic, Sara has another window: the skylight. This window is at the top of the house, and like the attic in which it is situated, it represents Sara's imagination at its most powerful; through the skylight Sara enters "another world," a world that makes "the things which were happening in the world below" seem "almost unreal" (100). The echo here is of George MacDonald's *At the Back of the North Wind,* in which windows figure prominently, especially in chapter 30, "Nanny's Dream." I might also cite MacDonald's comment that "the cellars are the metaphysics, the garrets the poetry of the house," from his novel *Malcolm* (1875). Also through the skylight comes Ram Dass and the beautiful things he brings to change Sara's dingy room into a felicitous space and to prepare her for a return to fortune and domestic security with Mr. Carrisford.

To return to the cab at the beginning of the novel, I should point out that as Sara sits beside her father she thinks of "the voyage she had just made from Bombay." The thought of this voyage does not, however, bring her the thrill of adventure; instead, she shrinks from all the strangeness of her recent experiences and moves "closer to her father" (7). Sara does not desire adventure, outside of books, and she does not desire independence. As we saw earlier, she desires nothing more than to serve her father, to keep his house. She thinks neither of having a career nor of accomplishing deeds of public value, and she attains something close to her heart's desire when she becomes friends with Mr. Carrisford.

But this is not entirely fair. The book does associate Sara with domestic things—homes and hearths and windows—but she also comes to know the city. Her first introduction to London is her arrival at Miss Minchin's Select Seminary, "a big, dull, brick house, exactly like all the others in its row" (9–10). The house is not in fashionable London; its situation in a dingy square is the first indication that the city might have a dark side. The house itself, as the narrator makes clear, is like its owner: "respectable and well-furnished" but ugly. *Hard, severe, heavy,* and *square* are words that describe both the house and Miss Minchin. They might also describe the London Sara comes to know during her period of adversity. The city is severe in its treatment of the dispossessed or those whom Sara calls the "populace." Similarly, Miss Minchin is severe on those who have no money and position. She goes so far as to say outright that Becky is not to be considered human. When Sara tells Miss Minchin that "Becky is a little girl too," Miss Minchin replies, "Becky is the scullery-maid. Scullery maids—er—are not little girls." To drive the point home, the narrator informs the reader that it "had not occurred to her to think of them in that light. Scullery-maids were machines who carried coal-scuttles and made fires" (67).

What we have in Miss Minchin is an independent woman who fears economic hardship. Consequently, she thinks of nothing other than her pocketbook. To her, ownership is power, and ownership comes from having money. What Burnett touches on here is the necessity of money and the effect this necessity has on people who must work for a living and who have pretensions to position within the social hierarchy. Obviously the woman who runs the bakeshop is unlike Miss Minchin; she pretends to no fashionable lifestyle and she has sympathy for others less prosperous than herself. More prosperous still is Mr. Carmichael, a lawyer who can maintain a London house and provide for his wife, eight children, a grandmother, and "any number of servants" (111). Wealthier still is Mr. Carrisford, who need not work now that his investments in India have made him independent. Sara's father, too, had been very rich, but just how he came into his money remains unspoken. The message in all this is, however, that the world functions as an economic system. Men find position and wealth in the professions or in business; women run shops or schools, and if they wish to remain in polite society they marry and keep the home.

When Sara becomes indigent she runs errands for Miss Minchin and her staff. These take her into London's byways, and she sees something of real poverty and want. The young girl, Anne, to whom Sara gives her freshly baked buns is reminiscent of child waifs from Dickens—say, Want and Ignorance from *A Christmas Carol* (1843). The experience of London's poor reveals how confining the city can be, and Sara's desire to "feed the populace" is a desire to transform the mean streets of London into something closer to the shining streets she tells Lottie about when she speaks of Lottie's mother and heaven (see 47). Although we have no information to take us beyond Sara's restored fortune and new home with Mr. Carrisford it is significant that the book ends not in Mr. Carrisford's house but with Sara's trip to the bakeshop and her meeting with Anne, now employed in the shop. The two share a moment of unspoken understanding, and the reader might leave the book feeling that Sara will continue her quest to feed the poor and improve conditions in the city. We might take Sara's good works as typical of the charity activity of many middle-class Victorian women, and dismiss these good works as based on convention rather than conviction, but the book sustains a different reading. Sara's fall into poverty and want has given her a mission to participate in the social revolution that was beginning to take place in England in the late nineteenth century with the founding of the Socialist League and the Working Man's Movement. I use the word *mission* precisely because it conjures up an image of Empire—the mission to the colonies, missionaries and their activities among the "natives." Sara's mission is to repatriate the activities of Empire, and in doing this she implicitly offers a criticism of imperial activity abroad.

11

Shining Streets, Fields of Lilies, and God's Creatures

When Sara speaks to Lottie of heaven's shining streets, she also speaks of fields of lilies. To the little girl who lives in a dull brick house in a dingy square in foggy London, this is a reminder of nature's beauty and freshness. Readers of Burnett's most famous book, *The Secret Garden,* will know how important nature is to her. The garden, the robin, Dickon's animals, and even the wide moor itself bring fresh air and health to the two deprived and unhealthy children, Mary and Colin. Burnett's memoir, *The One I Knew the Best of All,* also testifies to her love of nature, as does her life-long interest in gardening. We might, then, ask about the role of nature in *A Little Princess.*

A Little Princess is a city book, but nature is present and important in Sara Crewe's life. As in most children's books, the good child has an instinctive attachment to and understanding of nature. Finding something positive in her diminished position, Sara shows Lottie her rooftop world with its friendly sparrows. These sparrows become Sara's friends: "when she stood upon the table, put her head and shoulders out of the attic window, and chirped, she heard almost immediately a flutter of wings and answering twitters, and a little flock of dingy town birds appeared and alighted on the slates to talk to her and make much of the crumbs she scattered" (115). She describes what she sees from her bed when she looks through the skylight at the visible patch of sky: "If the sun is going to shine, little pink clouds float about, and I feel as if I could touch them. And if it rains, the drops patter and patter as if they were saying something nice. Then if there are stars, you can lie and try to count how many got into the patch." Her attic, she concludes, "is almost like a nest in a tree" (102).

The near simile ("almost like") of the nest becomes a full-fledged symbol in *The Secret Garden,* used to underscore the connection between the children and the natural world and to suggest the importance of natural growth for the children. In *A Little Princess* the nest informs us that the attic is not so bad a place that Sara cannot grow and mature there; in fact, she can and does. And as if to emphasize the naturalness of this nest, Burnett brings Sara into contact with two creatures from the animal world: the rat, Melchisedec, and the monkey who escapes from Ram Dass. Both of these animals function as signs of Sara's kinship with displaced and marginal characters.

At first the thought of rats and mice makes Sara tremble, but when a rat does confront her, what she perceives differs from her first thoughts. The rat who has come to get some crumbs dropped by Lottie "looked so queer and so like a grey-whiskered dwarf or gnome that Sara was rather fascinated" (104). The similes show Sara's imagination at work, and imagination is the mental faculty that allows us to sympathize with others. The key word here is *queer,* one of Burnett's favorite words, always used as a compliment. Sara herself is *queer,* and the word thus draws a kinship between the rat and the little girl. Sara muses: "I dare say it is rather hard to be a rat," and she places herself in the rat's situation: "Nobody likes you. People jump and run away and scream out: 'Oh, a horrid rat!' I shouldn't like people to scream and jump and say: 'Oh, a horrid Sara!' the moment they saw me, and set traps for me, and pretend they were dinner. It's so different to be a sparrow. But nobody asked this rat if he wanted to be a rat when he was made. Nobody said: 'Wouldn't you rather be a sparrow?'" (104). Sara here expresses something akin to Keats's notion of "the poetical Character itself," which has a great capacity for imaginative identification with others. Burnett, like her romantic precursors in their most ideal moments, has an essentialist ethic. All things partake of the same spirit in a world made in harmony, if only we can recognize this.

The narrator describes the rat as if it were human, an echo of personification that goes at least as far back as Sarah Trimmer's *Fabulous Histories* or *The History of the Robins* (1786). Sara's rat is the head of a large family that lives in the wall, and he has "left the children crying bitterly" (133). Sara decides she will befriend him, and accordingly she makes overtures to him. The narrator then expresses the essentialist ethic I mentioned above: "How is it that animals understand things I do not know, but it is certain that they do understand. Perhaps there is a language which is not made of words and everything in the world understands it. Perhaps there is a soul hidden in everything and it can always speak, without even making a sound, to another soul" (104–5). I am reminded in this passage of Wordsworth's sense sublime that rolls through all things and in the mind of man. In any case, Burnett's narrator expresses a belief in an ineffable truth too deep for words yet active in the universe. The language "not made of words" recurs at the end of the novel when Sara and Anne "looked straight into each other's eyes" (224).

Sara explains to Ermengarde that the rat "*is* a person. . . . He gets hungry and frightened, just as we do; and he is married and has children" (108). Burnett's respect for the animal world, her sense that creatures connect in some spiritual way is perhaps best illustrated when she allows the rat the status of a focalizing character. This occurs in chapter 14, "What Melchisedec Heard and Saw," in which Melchisedec scurries away when he hears a noise on the roof. From his hole in the wall, he watches as Ram Dass and another young man scrutinize the room and make notes concerning what needs to be done to transform it into a felicitous space. The chapter is reminiscent of a chapter in *The Secret Garden* in which the reader follows the action in the garden from the point of view of the robins.

The difference between the respective passages in the two books rests on the difference between robins and rats. Clearly, the robins (and the sparrows in *A Little Princess*) allow Burnett to suggest things spiritual because of the traditional association of birds with spirit. Rats, however, have quite other associations. The rat is the bringer of the plague, a harbinger of death, and a thing of darkness. Like E. B. White in *Charlotte's Web,* Burnett asks us to reevaluate the importance of rats and to consider them with some sympathy as creatures like ourselves. Unlike the robins in *The Secret Garden,* however, Melchisedec does not guide the reader's attitudes toward the main character or characters. Instead, Melchisedec reflects the reader's sense of wonder at the goings on in the attic room while Sara is absent. In other words, Melchisedec represents the reader who remains "greatly mystified" at the activities of Ram Dass and the young secretary.

From the opposite perspective, the reader adopts Sara's attitude toward Melchisedec and accepts him as one of God's creatures. The knowing reader has yet another perspective from which to view the rat; this is the view provided by Sara's naming the creature Melchisedec. We know already from the stories Sara tells Lottie about heaven that Sara has a knowledge of the Bible, but her choice of name for the rat also shows this. Melchisedec is an Old Testament type of priest-king, a precursor of Christ. The Hebrew word *malki-sedeq* means "king of righteousness." Just why Sara chooses this name for the rat remains unspoken, but the name conjures up thoughts of bread and wine, of sanctuary, generosity, and blessings. Mechisedec is a type, and as a type he is "without father, without mother, without descent, having neither beginning of days, nor end of life" (Heb. 7:3). Just as Sara sees her rat as a type of Christ, she sees herself as a type of woman, the fairy-tale princess.

This use of types raises interesting questions regarding the construction of subjectivity in the novel. Ostensibly, the acceptance of a type of person—princess, priest-king, soldier, scullery maid, and so forth—suggests an acceptance of human subjectivity as essential, something we are born to and not something we are made into. This notion of an essential subjectivity used to be called "human nature." In terms of fairy-tale characters, we have princesses and wicked witches, one representing human nature at its finest—gentle, honest, loving, and kind—and the other human nature at its worst—harsh, deceiving, brutal, and greedy. From their different perspectives, both Miss Minchin and Sara accept the notion of human nature as essential. Miss

Minchin's idea of class reflects her notion that birth makes the person, and so does Sara's belief that she and Becky are the same, "only two little girls—just two little girls" (86). Becky's response to Sara's claim that she and Becky are the same complicates the issue of human nature, and I will return to the problem later when I discuss the book's narrator and narrative construction.

Now, however, I turn to the other signifier of nature: the monkey. Just as Sara befriends the rat, so, too, she befriends the monkey. Her way with animals signifies her goodness, her closeness to nature, her natural sympathy for the creatures of the earth, among whom Burnett numbers the poor and disenfranchised. In other words, the monkey serves Burnett for another perspective on humanity as much as it allows her to show a kindly attitude to nature. Just as Sara considers Melchisedec human, so, too, does Ram Dass consider the monkey human. The narrator tells us that Ram Dass knew the monkey "as if he were his child" (125). And later in the novel Burnett allows the monkey to focalize the action. When he comes to Sara's room one night, she coaxes him in: "He knew she would not hurt him. He knew it before she laid her soft, caressing little paw on him and drew him toward her" (196). The monkey perceives Sara as an animal, just as she perceives him in terms of a human, wondering whether he has a mind (197).

Sara protects and mothers the monkey just as she mothers characters such as Lottie and Emily. From another perspective, however, both the monkey and Sara are displaced creatures. Burnett implicitly draws a comparison between the monkey, Ram Dass, and Sara. All three are lonely, far from home, and in need of companionship. Sara feels an instinctive kinship with Ram Dass the first time she sees him peeking over the roofs of nearby houses: "The first thing she thought was that his dark face looked sorrowful and homesick. She felt absolutely sure he had come up to look at the sun, because he had seen it so seldom in England that he longed for a sight of it. She looked at him interestedly for a second, and then smiled across the slates. She had learned to know how comforting a smile, even from a stranger, may be" (124). Sara's first instinct is to see Ram Dass as someone who expresses similar feelings to herself: sorrow and homesickness. As for Ram Dass, he, too, feels akin to Sara, telling the young secretary that "we are both lonely"

(203). Burnett's position here, as elsewhere in the novel, appears to embrace a liberal humanist ethic that sees everyone as partaking of an essential humanity that transcends class, cultural, and racial differences.

As we might expect, however, Burnett is not consistent. Ram Dass, like the monkey, is not similar to Sara. Far from it. And Ram Dass knows this. He speaks to the "Missee Sahib" "as if he were speaking to the little daughter of a rajah" (126). He is "respectful" and claims to be Sara's "servant." In other words, class and race separate the little girl and the Indian man. Burnett does not allow the reader to forget that Ram Dass is a "native Indian" (124). As such, Ram Dass has more in common with the monkey than he does with Sara. He crosses from his window to Sara's "as steadily and lightly as if he had walked on roofs all his life," and he returns "with as much agility as the monkey himself had displayed" (126). Ram Dass remains, in the eyes of Northern Europeans in the novel, a representative of the "other," that which differs from the norm of humanity. To the young secretary, "Only an Oriental could have planned" the transformation of Sara's attic room (156), and to Mr. Carrisford the same transformation "could not have been done" without "the help of an agile, soft-footed Oriental like Ram Dass" (202). Despite Burnett's desire to present Ram Dass sympathetically, she cannot overcome her sense of his difference; she cannot present him other than stereotypically.

All things in nature, then, are not equal. Perhaps the displacement of Emily, the doll, by Boris, the boarhound, at the end of the novel nicely brings Burnett's attitude toward nature to a close. Sara is continuously compared to a fairy-tale princess, and as such she transcends nature. She might be called preternatural. In any case, as a special person Sara deserves nature's obeisance; nature's function is to serve the little princess. This explains the inscription on Boris's gold collar: "I serve the Princess Sara" (296). The dog not only displaces the doll, but also the rat and the monkey. In the hierarchy of nature's creatures, a dog is, we might remember, man's (or in this case a young girl's) best friend.

12

King Laugh

I take my title for this chapter from a book published eight years before *A Little Princess:* Bram Stoker's *Dracula* (1897). This may seem a strange book for me to draw on, as it has little in common with Burnett's children's book aside from a generic relationship to romance. It does, however, give prominent place to laughter, and laughter is also important to Burnett. Without laughter life is dreary and relationships are difficult to establish. Even more, without laughter life may become intolerable. Life's sweet mystery might well be the ability of the human being to laugh; life's bitter mystery might well be palatable only through laughter.

In *Dracula* the Dutchman Van Helsing commits what we might take to be an extreme act of indecorum, even rank thoughtlessness, when he laughs at the funeral of Lucy Westenra. Lucy has died under strange circumstances, and several strong men have tried valiantly but vainly, by giving of their blood, to keep her alive. Van Helsing is the only character who has any idea as to the truth of her mysterious death; she has died by the bite of a vampire, and her destiny is to become one of the living dead. Van Helsing's knowledge of this is knowledge of hideous evil; more, it is a knowledge of a deep and abiding evil in the world destroying innocence and purity. To make matters worse, Van Helsing knows that most people are immune from such knowledge because of its very enormity; the human mind cannot take in such a seemingly irrational and inexplicable evil. Just as we cannot look at God's face and live, so, too, we cannot look at the face of ultimate evil and remain sane. The only thing we can do to cope with this unbearable knowledge is to laugh.

Obviously Van Helsing's laughter is not directly similar to laughter in *A Little Princess,* but his notion of what he calls "King Laugh" is relevant to our understanding of Burnett's vision. King Laugh is a safety valve allowing us to overcome extreme stress in order to get on with the labor of living. Van Helsing puts it this way: "But King Laugh he come like the sunshine, and he ease off the strain again; and we bear to go on with our labour, what it may be."[31] A little laughter is not a dangerous thing; it is necessary if we are to bear life's slings and arrows. Take, for example, Captain Crewe with his "splitting headache . . . in his bungalow in India." He sits at a table upon which are "papers and letters which were alarming him and filling him with anxious dread," but when he reads a letter from his daughter Sara, "he laughed as he had not laughed in weeks" (63). The narrator does not tell us that this laughter relieves his anxiety, but we must conclude that it does. Why else mention it?

In *A Little Princess* laughter brings a little sunshine into Sara's gloomy life in the attic; it brings people together as we see when Ermengarde visits Sara. The two girls huddle together and tell each other things, and Sara hugs her knees and laughs as she listens to her friend (163). A little later the two girls hear Miss Minchin scolding Becky at the top of the stairs, just outside Sara's room. Sara's anger mounts as Miss Minchin mistakenly accuses Becky of stealing and then slaps her. Ermengarde suddenly realizes just how difficult a life Sara herself endures. To find something positive in her life, Sara tells Ermengarde that a small boy once gave her "a sixpence for charity." Then she shows Ermengarde this same sixpence, and the sight of it "made them laugh a little, though they both had tears in their eyes" (167). Sara has a habit of emitting a "little laugh" (52, 106, 114, 129, 142, 170), which signals her indomitable spirit.

Sara's indomitable spirit, as manifested by her laugh, has a biblical source. Despite the alteration of spelling, we can expect that the name Sara echoes that of the Old Testament matriarch Sarah, a name that in Hebrew means "princess." Sarah is Abraham's wife, the mother of Isaac ("he laughs") and "a mother of nations" (Gen. 17:16). Throughout her life Sarah is barren, but when she is 90 years old she learns that she is to have a child. Her response is to laugh, and for this God rebukes her (Gen. 18: 12–15). Sure enough, a year later Sarah gives birth to a son. Sarah's reaction is joy, and she reminds us of her laughter: "God hath made me to laugh, so that all who hear will laugh with me" (Gen. 21: 6). This laughter is life-affirming.

And this affirmation is something Sara can pass on to others. Early in the book she makes friends with Becky, the scullery maid. Becky's life has not left her much joy; she is nervous and hesitant. The narrator tells us that she "had scarcely known what laughter was through all her poor, little hard-driven life" (62). Her first meeting with Sara introduces her to Sara's "little laugh," and the two become friends. Sara, whom the narrator calls "a giver" by nature (62), gives Becky, among other things, "help and comfort and laughter." Sometimes, the narrator tells us, "kind laughter is the best help of all" (62). The two girls laugh together, and their laughter "was as 'fillin' as the meat-pies" Sara bought for Becky. People can, it seems, live without bread, but not without laughter.

Another way of putting this might be to say that laughter is liberating; it allows at least a momentary respite from care and even hunger. Liberating laughter breaks down barriers: the scullery maiden and the "little princess" come together, or, in the case of Ermengarde and Sara, the clever and the dull come together. Laughter levels. It creates a true community. It also challenges authority. The power of laughter lies in its effective dismantling of power. One scene in the novel illustrates this clearly. Sara has finished giving the younger pupils their French lesson, and as she puts the books away she thinks of "the various things royal personages in disguise were called upon to do." Of course, her reverie reflects her sense of her own identity as a "princess-in-rags." She thinks of Alfred the Great and the story of the burnt cakes. In the story Alfred, in disguise, visits a countrywoman's cottage and agrees to watch some cakes that are baking. The countrywoman, called a neat-herd (a person who looks after cattle), leaves the cottage, and while she's gone Alfred falls asleep. When the woman returns to find her cakes burned, she strikes the man, not realizing who he is. When Sara thinks of this story, her face takes on the look Miss Minchin hates to see. Outraged, Miss Minchin "actually flew at her and boxed her ears—exactly as the neat-herd's wife had boxed King Alfred's." For a second, Sara stands still; then "she broke into a little laugh" (129).

The "little laugh" reflects Sara's resistance to Miss Minchin's authority. Miss Minchin has no sense of humor whatsoever, and to hear Sara laugh simply enrages her. Although he writes about a far different cultural context—medieval carnival—Mikhail Bakhtin describes laughter in ways pertinent to its presentation in *A Little Princess.* In *Rabelais and His World* Bakhtin stresses the regenerative and healing aspects of laughter.[32] It expresses liberation from fear and authority, from power and prohibition, and it is "also related to food and drink," to festivity (95). The carnival that Bakhtin describes is a festival of inversion and subversion; it overturns normal regulations and strict laws of behavior policed by state authority. During carnival, the oppressed become, for a moment anyway, the free and joyful. The time of carnival is a time of anti-authority and egalitarianism. In its own way, what I have just outlined describes the "royal feast" Sara and her friends have in the attic in chapter 15. What Bakhtin calls "carnival," Sara calls "the Magic" (169). If you pretend enough, anything can happen, including the transformation of a barren attic room into a banquet hall.

Laughter, then, is connected with the spirit of pretend, which in turn is connected to play. Burnett writes about children who work—Sara runs errands and does other work about the house, Becky is a scullery maid, the children in *The Secret Garden* work in the garden, the boys in *The Lost Prince* work for the exiled government—but she does not forget the importance of play to a developing child. Indeed, work that has no component of play in it must be drudgery, antihuman, and counterproductive. Sara's work is such drudgery; it is not in the least like the healthy gardening of the children in *The Secret*

Garden, nor even like the serious "game" of undercover espionage played by Marco and the Rat in *The Lost Prince.* The only means Sara has of dealing with the drudgery of her existence is to indulge her imagination—in other words, to play fanciful games. She fancies herself a hostess in her attic, entertaining Ermengarde, and she thinks,

> If I lived in a castle . . . and Ermengarde was the lady of another castle, and came to see me, with knights and squires and vassals riding with her, and pennons flying; when I heard the clarions sounding outside the drawbridge I should go down to receive her, and I should spread feasts in the banquet-hall and call in minstrels to sing and play and relate romances. When she comes into the attic I can't spread feasts, but I can tell stories, and not let her know disagreeable things. I dare say poor chatelaines had to do that in times of famine, when their lands had been pillaged. (163–64)

As the narrator says, Sara is a "brave little chatelaine" dispensing the largesse of her mind to Becky and Ermengarde. In naming Sara a chatelaine, the narrator is complicit with the girls in their game of romance. The girls pretend their attic room is a banquet hall in a castle, and Ermengarde provides food from the box of goodies she has received from her aunt. Soon the three girls are pretending to have a feast and laughing joyfully together. Friendship, trust, and the willingness to share both food and ideas are important here. The three girls—one the daughter of a well-to-do father, another an orhpan recently become destitute, and the third a scullery maid—form a community of equals. Almost despite her deep-seated class consciousness, Burnett has created a true female support group that includes members from both ends of the social spectrum.

What Burnett wants to communicate to her readers is the importance of such support groups. I suspect that her presentation of Sara and Mr. Carrisford at the end of the novel is intended to illustrate how what I am calling "support groups" can and ought to cross barriers of gender and age as earlier in the attic they crossed class barriers. Mr.

Carrisford and Sara support each other: "There were never such friends as these two became. Somehow, they seemed to suit each other in a wonderful way" (220). From her group of three in the attic, Sara has come to a group of two. But not quite. The novel ends, as we have seen before, with Sara's return to the bakeshop, where she meets for a second time Anne, the former beggar child and now a shop employee. The suggestion that both Sara and Anne will do their part to feed "the populace" suggests the need for support to go beyond closed communities of home and school. By the story's end, the laughter of young girls has receded, replaced by the thoughtful smiles of maturity. Stories of knights, squires, and vassals now become the real story of two girls whose quest is to give bread and buns to needy children.

13

Narrative Voice

Much of what I have written deals with the book's themes: imagination, laughter, social conditions of the time, the importance of nature, and growing up. I have also noticed some images: the doll, the house, and the city. Mostly, I have been dealing with the story, the action of the novel, what happens to the characters. No reading would be complete, however, without some consideration of the narrative discourse—that is, the way in which the story is told. Obviously, no one way exists for an author to tell a story, as the existence of the play version of *A Little Princess* reveals. An author has choices to make in the way he or she tells a story, and in *A Little Princess* Burnett chooses to use a third-person narrator to tell the story. She sets up what narratologists call an "authorial narrative situation."[33] That is, she uses a narrator who is omniscient, who is not a participant in the events, and who knows more than any of the characters know. For example, when Sara learns of the death of her father, she runs to her room, then shuts and locks the door. The narrator tells us:

> Nobody but Sara herself ever knew what had happened in her room after she had run upstairs and locked her door. In fact, she

> herself scarcely remembered anything but that she walked up and down, saying over and over again to herself in a voice which did not seem her own:
>
> "My papa is dead! My papa is dead!"
>
> Once she stopped before Emily. (80–81)

The beginning of the last sentence above indicates that the narrator knows more than Sara knows about Sara's own movements.

This narrator is also omnipresent: he or she can move freely through time and space. When Sara writes to her father a few weeks before her eleventh birthday, she is living at Miss Minchin's while her father is back in India, but the narrator interrupts the narrative of life at school to switch the focus to Captain Crewe's bungalow in India, where the captain, suffering from a severe headache, reads a letter from his daughter and receives relief through laughter (63). The narrator has the power and authority to make such switches in place and to collapse time because he or she completely controls the action. Such a narrative point of view is familiar in traditional fictions, and it serves one very obvious purpose useful to writers of children's books: it provides the reader with the security of a single point of view. The narratological term for such single-voiced narratives is "monologic narrative" (Prince, 54). The reader, again, need not feel at a loss regarding what to think at any moment in the action because "the narrator's views, judgements, and knowledge constitute the ultimate authority with respect to the world represented" (54).

Ostensibly, then, Burnett's choice for her authorial narrative situation is straightforward. This does not mean, however, that it is simple. The reader of *A Little Princess* must be a competent reader, able to understand narrative conventions. Take, for example, the first paragraph of the novel: "Once on a dark winter's day, when the yellow fog hung so thick and heavy in the streets of London that the lamps were lighted and the shop windows blazed with gas as they do at night, an odd-looking little girl sat in a cab with her father, and was driven rather slowly through the big thorough-fares" (1). The adult reader might catch here a distant echo of Dickens's *Bleak House* with its similar opening on a dreary November day in which fog fills the air and shop windows are lighted two hours before their usual time. The conjunction of realism and romance occurs in *Bleak House,* too, with Dickens's allusions to Rip Van Winkle and Sleeping Beauty in the opening of chapter 2. The opening of *A Little Princess* reduces Dickens's long, lyrical, and rhetorically charged beginning to make it available to a young readership. What Burnett wants, however, is to echo the great Victorian novelist of social conditions who invested his narratives with echoes of fairy tales. The child reader of *A Little Princess* might sense the first echo in Burnett's novel of fairy tales in the opening phrasing: "Once on a dark winter's day." In this one phrase Burnett combines the fairy-tale echo with the theme of descent, darkness, and coldness that pervades the book's depicition of London life.

The competent reader will also note the theme of reversal in this opening paragraph. The time is "day," yet the gas lamps shine as if it were "night." The turning of day into night accomplished by the yellow fog prepares us for the turning of a little princess into a child drudge. Even the passive verb in the last sentence serves a purpose; it suggests, if ever so quietly, that Sara's destiny is out of her hands. Indeed, it is. Sara's destiny lies in the hands of the story's narrator, who controls everything within the narrative. So far, however, we have an unobtrusive narrator, one who merely recounts what happens or describes a place. The narrator begins to take on a stronger character when he or she (the narrator's gender is not specified, but for the sake of simplicity I shall refer to Burnett's narrator from now on as "she") notes in the second paragraph that the little girl "stared out of the window at the passing people with a queer old-fashioned thoughtfulness in her big eyes." This sets up the reader for the narrator's move into the girl's inner life.

First we should follow through with the idea of the book's monologic voice. Burnett's desire to present a controlled world, one in which unambiguous values are clearly evident, manifests itself in certain repeated verbal tags: "in fact," "To tell the truth," "The Truth was," "it was true," "really." The repeated use of such locutions makes it clear that the narrator has access to truth. She knows what happens, when it happens, what people think about what happens and about each other. This becomes apparent as early as the book's third paragraph:

> She was such a little girl that one did not expect to see such a look on her small face. It would have been an old look for a child of twelve, and Sara Crewe was only seven. The fact was, however, that she was always dreaming and thinking odd things, and could not herself remember any time when she had not been thinking things about grown-up people and the world they belonged to. She felt as if she had lived a long, long time. (7)

The first sentence here contains a curious use of the word *one*. Who is this "one"? The narrator speaks not only for herself but also for anyone. Anyone would have found the look on the little girl's face queerly "old-fashioned." The narrator assumes the authority to speak for all people who might see this girl. Then she tells the reader something about Sara's thought processes: she was always dreaming. Delving into Sara's thoughts, even in this vague way, allows the narrator to draw attention to the separation of child and adult. Children like Sara belong to one world; adults belong to another. We can assume that the narrator herself is an adult, an authoritative one. Finally, the narrator tells us what Sara feels.

Throughout the book the narrator shows the ability to know what characters think and feel. For example, when Miss Minchin learns that Sara can speak French and that she had tried to tell Miss Minchin this, she "felt infuriated." To make her knowledge of Miss Minchin more pointed, the narrator goes on to say that Miss Minchin "began from that minute to feel rather a grudge against her show pupil" (25; *show* here means a model student, one to use for publicity when visitors come to the school). The narrator's complete knowledge of both outer and inner events in the story is perhaps most obviously evident in chapter 14, "What Melchisedec Heard and Saw." In this chapter the narrator delves into the point of view of the rat, a technique that turns up in *The Secret Garden* in chapter 25, "The Curtain," when the point of view switches to that of the robins. The narrator in *A Little Princess* speaks of Melchisedec's feelings as fact: the attic is quiet, and "Melchisedec had, in fact, found it rather dull; and when the rain ceased to patter and perfect silence reigned, he decided to come out and reconnoitre" (152). Perhaps the silence does encourage the rat to come out, but how can we know whether he found the quiet attic "dull"?

In any case, what the narrator does here is to use one of the book's characters as a focalizer or point-of-view character. In narratological terms, *A Little Princess* contains a heterodiegetic narrator—a narrator who is not part of the events she recounts, who has access to the thoughts and feelings of the story's characters and who enters these thoughts and feelings whenever she wishes. Here is an example:

> Lavinia could not think of exactly the right thing to say. Several times she had found that she could not think of a satisfactory reply when she was dealing with Sara. The reason of this was that, somehow, the rest always seemed to be vaguely in sympathy with her opponent. She saw now that they were pricking up their ears interestedly. The truth was, they liked princesses, and they all hoped they might hear something more definite about this one, and drew nearer Sara accordingly. (59)

The tags "the reason for this" and "the truth was" indicate the authority of the narrator; she knows of what she speaks. She also focalizes both Lavinia and the other students.

This narrative authority is also apparent in the willingness of the narrator to speak in the form of dicta. For example, when Miss Minchin prepares to make a speech at Sara's eleventh birthday party, Sara feels "uncomfortable," and the narrator declares, "It is not agreeable to stand in a schoolroom and have a speech made about you" (68). And perhaps a more telling example occurs when the narrator informs us that Sara is, by nature, a giving person. She goes on to say, "If Nature has made you for a giver, your hands are born open, and so is your heart" (75). The tone of such pronouncements is confident and authoritative. The reader finds little necessity to work things out for herself; *A Little Princess,* in other words, is what Roland Barthes terms a "readerly text."

You might ask how this relates to the book's thematic concerns. Earlier I discussed the role of the Empire as background to this book, and if we think for a moment we will realize that the sustaining themes of Empire are power, authority, control, manipulation. To maintain an Empire, a ruling state must manage two things: to establish a right to authority and to perpetrate an overriding ideology or pattern of thinking that those within the influence of Empire accept as natural. We can see both these aspects of Empire in Burnett's handling of the narrative in *A Little Princess.* First, we have already seen how the narrator of the story assumes a position of authority through controlling the reader's response to characters and action. If we need a reminder, we might recall how she categorizes Captain Crewe as "a rash, innocent young man" (14), his daughter as "a very fine little person" (21), and Ermengarde as "the monumental dunce of the school" (28). The reader is never in doubt as to how to respond to the characters.

Second, I might expand on my last example: the narrator categorizes Ermengarde as "fat," "slow," "dull," and "stupid" (27). Although Ermengarde is a likable person and a friend of Sara's, the reader is never in any doubt about which of the two characters is the more worthy of admiration. Obviously, the reader is supposed to value Sara's reading habits and her active imagination, and to accept these as somehow better than Ermengarde's resistance to reading and sluggish imagination. That Ermengarde is "stupid" is a given. Although we know that Ermengarde lives in fear of her father who expects his daughter to read and understand all sorts of difficult books, and although we know that she is a "kind" person, the narrator never asks us to consider whether her relationship with her father has something to do with Ermengarde's slowness, her resistance to learning. In other words, Ermengarde's stupidity is something we take for granted, never questioning whether her failure to learn is natural or acquired.

This quiet inculcation of attitudes on the part of the narrator works its way into assumptions regarding both class and race. Note, for example, the beginning of the book, where the narrator describes Sara's privileged early life: "She had always lived in a beautiful bungalow, and had been used to seeing many servants who made salaams to her and called her 'Missee Sahib' and gave her her own way in everything" (8). Surrounded by opulence and people who satisfied her every wish, Sara never thinks about other people. Now this is most probable.

The narrator, however, goes on to say that Sara's only trouble in her early life was "'the place' she was to be taken to some day" (8). Having said this, the narrator adds, "The climate of India was very bad for children, and as soon as possible they were sent away from it—generally to England and to school" (8). As readers, we accept this information in a neutral way; the narrator has already drawn us in with her confident and knowledgeable voice. The sentence I quote simply prepares us for a necessary plot development—Sara's journey from India to England, where she will attend Miss Minchin's Select Seminary for Young Ladies.

The information regarding the deleterious effects of India's climate comes in a paragraph sequence in which the narrator focalizes the narrative through Sara; we have a peek at her thinking, but we also have the narrator's comments on her thinking: for example, we know that to Sara her "young, handsome, rich, petting father seemed to be the only relation she had in the world" (8). This passage presents Sara's thoughts regarding her relations, but it does so in a manner that suggests her thoughts are mediated by the narrator, who passes judgment on Captain Crewe's youth, looks, wealth, and fondness for his child. Sara is unlikely to think of her own father as "young" or "petting" for that matter. More to the point, however, is the narrator's comment that Sara "only knew" her father was rich "because she had heard people say so when they thought she was not listening" (8). My point is that the narrator, despite being outside the action of the story, insinuates herself into the telling in such a way that her presence is nearly always situated between the reader and the story's action and characters. The voice is strong, drawing on the oral storytelling techniques both Sara and her creator know so well. A clear instance of this occurs at the beginning of chapter 16, when the narrator addresses the reader directly: "Imagine, if you can, what the rest of the evening was like" (181).

The reader, then, does not question what happens in this story. The narrative voice comforts in its reassuring presence. When the narrator informs us that Miss Minchin's cook and housemaids are "not servants of the best class" (88), we believe her, and in so doing we accept differences in class both across the social spectrum and within one band. The result of such acceptance of conventional values of the time leads the reader not to question even the most egregious of the book's presumptions. Note, for example, the dialogue between Becky and Sara concerning the so-called Indian Gentleman who moves in next door to Miss Minchin's. Telling Sara about the "Nindian gentleman," Becky informs her that the man is a heathen: "He worships idols, miss. He's an 'eathen an' bows down to wood an' stone. I seen a' idol bein' carried in for him to worship. Somebody had oughter send him a trac'." Becky presumes the man is a heathen because of what she sees; in actuality, she knows nothing about this man. Correcting her, Sara remarks that "some people like to keep them [idols] to look at because they are interesting" (120). The narrator's only comment on this exchange is to note that Becky preferred to believe the new neighbor was a heathen because this idea was "much more romantic" than if he were "the ordinary kind of gentleman who went to church with a prayer-book" (120–21).

That the narrator uses the words "ordinary kind of gentleman" reinforces the "otherness" of someone from India. This is, as far as it goes, fine. People from India are not identical with people from England. But the narrator does not intervene to gloss Sara's comment regarding idols—the fact that some people keep them because they are interesting. What "interesting" means remains unexplained. And even more important is the presumption that anyone who has a religion other than Christianity is a "heathen."

In short, the narrative voice in *A Little Princess* nicely completes the book's themes of Empire, class, and the power of story. Like Sara herself, the narrator has the privilege of knowing things and constructing the world. Just as Sara, through her imaginative activity and optimism, makes good (magic) things happen, so, too, does the narrator control the destiny of her characters. It is not, the narrative seems to say, merely good luck that makes good things happen but the power of knowing when and how to speak, how to deport yourself, and how to persevere.

Approaches to Teaching

How we might teach *A Little Princess* depends, of course, on the age of students we have. My discussion of the book in the previous pages should offer much in the way of "approaches" to the college teacher. Depending on whether we want a "top-down" or a "bottom-up" approach in the classroom, we might begin by placing the book in the context of early-twentieth-century children's books—books by the likes of Kipling, Grahame, Nesbit, and Montgomery—or we might begin by asking students to give their response to the book. This last approach is especially useful with a book some students are likely to have read as children. This use of response, as U. C. Knoepflmacher's comments in his introduction to the MLA's *Teaching Children's Literature* (1992) suggest, might well surface a "creative tension" between "the emotional gratification furnished by wish fulfillment and make-believe" and "the more skeptical pleasures of intellectual or analytical discovery."[34]

Another way of putting this tension between two ways of reading—the emotional and the analytical—is for us to make conscious just what it is we do when we read and interpret. If we believe, for example, that reading is a subjective activity, and that our nonliterary as well as our literary experiences affect how we react to anything we read, then we might wish to concentrate on the aspects of *A Little Princess* that speak directly to the feelings of our students. A discussion, such as the one by Lynne Schwartz I looked at in chapter three, of a reader's continual return to this book or even to a reader's strong attachment to it, can yield interesting insights into both the book and the reading process. It would, for example, be of interest to tabulate the reaction of female readers and male readers of the book. Books were, and still are, marketed as "girls' books" or "boys' books," and the difference between the two kinds of books will become clearer than they might otherwise be if we compare just how male and female readers react to a book ostensibly for girls—*A Little Princess.* For comparison, an instructor might take a book contemporary with Burnett's, such as Kipling's *Stalky and Co.* (1899), and tabulate the responses of male and female students.

Instructors can, of course, take a more objective approach to the same issue. For example, we might look at the plot of *A Little Princess* with a view to seeing whether this is gender related. First, we might note the obvious: the connection between the plot of *A Little Princess* and that of the fairy tale "Cinderella." I take the generic "Cinderella" rather than either the Perrault or Grimm tale. The story follows the fortunes of the central character who comes to be known as "Cinderella" after her mother dies, her father remarries, and her stepmother and stepsisters make her life miserable. In other words, Cinderella begins life comfortably enough and secure in the love of her parents, only to fall into suffering. The period of suffering is also a period of learning, which in Perrault's version involves the fairy godmother who assists Cinderella in preparing for the ball. In whatever version we read, these preparations for the ball take place, and they include Cinderella's close connection to nature. Finally, Cinderella achieves a recovery of happiness when the Prince seeks her out and identifies her through the glass (or silver or whatever) shoe.

In brief, this plot takes the girl from security to insecurity and back to security. Although not strictly speaking an orphan, Cinderella is the next thing to an orphan: her mother is dead and her father is ineffectual, even uncaring. A journey of sorts takes place when Cinderella goes three times to the king's ball. Cinderella's reward for her beauty, perseverance, and, most interesting of all, her disobedience (she stays too long at the ball on the third night necessitating an abrupt departure during which she loses her shoe) is marriage to the prince. This skeletal outline of the plot fits neatly onto *A Little Princess.* At the beginning of the novel Sara Crewe is comfortable and secure in her relationship with her father, and even after he leaves her at a school in London she remains comfortable and well cared for. Soon, however, her father dies, leaving her an orphan in penury, and the period of suffering ensues. Sara, like Cinderella, takes short journeys; hers are into the London streets to carry out errands for her employer. She becomes the object of interest to the man next door, who first lavishes on her, anonymously, presents of one kind and another. Finally, Sara's identity becomes known to this man, and he takes her into his house, out of the place of suffering and drudgery. Sara, like Cinderella, is rewarded for her beauty, perseverance, and disobedience (she disobeys Miss Minchin several times, including the time she, Ermengarde, and Becky have their "banquet" in the attic, and the time in the schoolroom when Miss Minchin chides Sara for thinking).

We might relate this plot to the standard, indeed archetypal, fairy-tale plot in which a hero sets out on a journey either to recover something or to prove something, runs into much harship, overcomes adversity, faces a monster of some sort in a great battle, and emerges triumphant. I refer, of course, to the standard plot of romance as outlined by Northrop Frye and others (see, for example, Frye's *The Secular Scripture*). The journey is shorthand for a fall and is often highlighted by a corresponding fall in nature, depicted through setting, either season or weather. In *A Little Princess* the city setting serves as a reminder of the main character's fall from innocence, and so, too, does the weather that is often wet and chilly. Indeed, the book opens in winter, announcing at the outset the theme of descent. The end of the plot brings an ascent that shows the hero achieving his or her goal, usually something that indicates a return to harmony and security. In *A Little Princess,* Sara's treasure (her father's fortune) is hers once again, and she has regained a father figure. She is also not only recognized as the little princess she has always been, but she has the power to spread "largesse" to the people. Much of this we have already seen.

If we compare Burnett's use of the fairy-tale or romance pattern with several other examples, we might learn something about the differences between a female and a male version of the standard plot. For example, we might read such fairy stories as "The Gallant Tailor," "Faithful John," or "Jack and the Beanstalk" alongside *A Little Princess.*

Or we might read some male-authored novels contemporary with Burnett: Stevenson's *Treasure Island,* Twain's *Huckleberry Finn,* or Andrew Lang's *Prince Prigio* (1889) and its sequel, *Prince Ricardo of Pantouflia* (1893). These stories and novels chronicle male quests for treasure, freedom, or a maiden. Whereas Sara and her precursor Cinderella take short and eddying journeys, the males travel far and wide. The world is truly before the males; the females do not get far away from house and home. Also, the males in the stories I mention are active; they make things happen. The females, on the other hand, are passive; things happen to them. In any case, my point is that this kind of comparison between male and female versions of the romance plot is a useful pedagogic strategy.

Although I have offered here examples of books written for young readers, another valuable activity might be the study of a work like *A Little Princess* alongside works for adults, either by Burnett herself or by her contemporaries. For example, Phyllis Bixler has noted the close connection between *A Little Princess* and *The Making of a Marchioness,* and I have noted the connection Burnett herself makes between the heroine of her children's story and that in her novel *A Lady of Quality.* Again, following Bixler's lead, students might examine how the conventions of a popular novelist make their way into Burnett's children's book. Such an approach is especially useful here because at the time Burnett was writing the distinction between books for children and those for adults blurred in the adolescent years. We have instances of the same book being published in two editions, one for children and one for adults (see, for example, Evelyn Sharp's *The Making of a Schoolgirl* [1899]). Just how does *A Little Princess* differ from *The Making of a Marchioness?*

For instructors of a historical bent, a study of the social context of *A Little Princess* might be of value. I have mentioned the backdrop of Imperial England, and students might explore the role of the British contingency in India during the nineteenth century. As a sidelight to this, a class might view the 1939 film of *A Little Princess* and discuss this in the context of the Boer War. And the class could make a comparison at quite another level with the treatment of the Boer conflict in the more recent Australian film, *Breaker Morant* (1979). Of course, more overtly Imperial books will provide an even more direct commentary on England's relationship to its colonies at the turn of the century; I refer to works by such writers as G. A. Henty, Bessie Marchant, and Kipling. And now we have the 1995 film that takes place during World War I; this film, too, offers much in the way of historical interest.

Students in North America might usefully work on the social context of Burnett's book. Clearly, Burnett's world is deeply and complexly based on class: the aristocratic class, business class, middle class, servant class, working class, and, at the very bottom, the destitute street people. All these are visible in *A Little Princess,* and students can learn how a society values its people based on such things as birth, money, position, merit, and so forth. This approach is not only useful from a historical point of view but also from a formal one. It allows the teacher to introduce a deconstructive reading. This means that it allows us to show how the book's consistency, its unity, breaks down. Traditional classroom approaches to literary works have focused on their unity of theme, setting, character development, and so on. The idea was that the work of art was a perfect harmony and impressed the reader with the completeness of its design.

Recent trends in literary criticism, however, have pointed out that anything created in language has a tendency to loosen, if not completely break down. Here's an example from *A Little Princess.* Ostensibly, this novel presents the reader with an egalitarian vision. Sara tells Becky early in the novel that the two of them are just the same: "we are just the same—I am only a little girl like you. It's just an accident that I am not you, and you are not me" (52). She repeats this after she learns of her father's death and her loss of fortune: "Oh, Becky . . . I told you we were just the same—only two little girls—just two little girls. You see how true it is. There's no difference now. I'm not a princess any more" (86). Now you must know that the narrator has before this reinforced the notion that a difference does exist between Sara and Becky. And she has done this in both subtle and not so subtle ways. On many occasions the narrator refers to the servant class, and she speaks of Becky as "an ugly, stunted, worn-out little scullery drudge" (49). When Sara first speaks to Becky, the narrator adds in a condescending tone that Sara speaks "quite as if she had been speaking to a little girl like herself" (51–52). The reader, however, has no doubts that Sara is of a different order of being from Becky. Indeed, as the narrator says, "Sara seemed as much unlike her [Becky] as if she were a creature from another world" (49). She is!

Consequently, when Becky replies to Sara's assertion that she is no longer a princess by saying, "Yes, miss, you are. . . . Whats'ever 'appens to you—whats'ever—you'd be a princess all the same—an' nothin' couldn't make you nothin' different" (86), the reader must concur with Becky. In short, Burnett's vision of an egalitarian society, best exemplified by the coterie of friends associated with the attic—Sara, Becky, Ermengarde, Lottie, and the assorted creatures (rats, sparrows, and monkey)—is undercut by her clear acceptance of the social divisions of her day. This kind of analysis, which looks for contradictions in the text, might be extended into other areas as well, such as the presentation of the female or the fashioning of the self.

Another context, one already noted earlier, has to do with the feminist movement at the turn of the century. "Feminist movement" is perhaps not the correct term, but students might usefully place *A Little Princess* in the context of women's writing in the late nineteenth century. The shift from emphasis on the angel in the house or household fairy to home goddess, as articulated in Judith Rowbotham's *Good Girls Make Good Wives* (1989), will provide a good start. Using as documentary evidence fiction for girls and women in the late Victorian period, Rowbotham shows how the shift from the ideal of the passive and house-bound woman to one more educated and capable of working outside the home took place. Clearly, Burnett's own life illustrates the widening sphere of women, and a reading of her work against other women writers of the time—Olive Schreiner, May Baldwin, Evelyn Everett Green, L. T. Meade, Mary Molesworth, and so forth—will prove instructive. Also, students might compare women writers with male writers who focus on women; I think of such writers as George DuMaurier, George Moore, George Gissing, George Meredith. Perhaps we have a conspiracy of Georges here!

Still, on a cultural note but closer to the politics of Empire is Burnett's sympathy with what she calls in *A Little Princess* "the populace." The pieces in Burnett's *Children I Have Known* (the U.S. title is *Giovanni and the Other* [1892]) contain a character identified as "the Socialist." One of the pieces, "The Boy Who Became a Socialist" (117–27), further identifies the Socialist as Burnett's young son, Vivian, and it explains that the influence of Edward Bellamy's novel *Looking Backward* (1888) turned the young lad to socialism. Burnett's own attitude to socialism seems somewhat less than committed; she pokes gentle fun at her serious-minded son. Yet Vivian's youthful enthusiasm is not out of step with his time. Books with utopian visions dependent on a socialist ideal were common at the turn of the century; a few examples include William Morris's *The Dream of John Ball* (1888) and *News from Nowhere* (1891), and H. G. Wells's *A Modern Utopia* (1905). In 1884 the first meeting of the Fabian Society took place, and in the same decade the Socialist League was founded. The period also saw the impact of the Arts and Crafts Movement begun somewhat earlier by William Morris and Company. The entire context of socialist thought might usefully form the basis for the study of books like *A Little Princess.* Is Burnett truly in sympathy with "the populace," or does she simply use the plot device of Sara, the "princess," showing her condescension to those below her on the social scale? Another question students might consider is whether Burnett is a serious writer or whether she simply latches onto ideas and symbols of her cultural moment. To answer this question, students might wish to return to Burnett's adult books—books such as *A Lady of Quality* and *The Making of a Marchioness,* which are to some extent parodic. How does Burnett's penchant for parody manifest itself in her children's books, and in *A Little Princess* particularly?

Obviously, several approaches to the book are possible. Just which approach one uses will depend, of course, on what the objectives of a particular class are. Teachers who wish to use the book with younger children—say, those between the ages of 11 and 15 (Burnett's primary audience)—might well consider the same areas of inquiry. Projects that involve historical research are possible. More often, however, books taught to children are presented in more intrinsic ways. By this I mean that the teaching of literature to children has traditionally focused on formal matters—close reading. Useful suggestions for presenting books to children in this way are available in many publications, for example David Jackson's *Encounters with Books: Teaching Fiction 11–16* (1983). On the other hand, Burnett herself has implicitly offered teachers a way into her book by writing her dramatized version of the story. Role-playing, dramatic readings, and full-fledged productions of the story are all possible. I myself am interested in the various illustrated versions of the text, and students might compare several of these, and even try their own hands at illustrating the story. And, of course, a comparison of the film versions with their written counterpart is something very relevant to the students' own world since reception of stories so often comes, in the first instance, on film these days.

Whatever approach an instructor takes or whatever activities a teacher plans for the teaching of this book, the important thing is to keep alive a work from our past that still speaks to us. Where we are in cultural development owes something to works such as *A Little Princess,* and we do well to keep this in mind. I end with the words of the anonymous reader who wrote so eloquently inside the front cover of my second-hand paperback copy of the book: "This is an excellent book!"

Notes and References

1. Vivian Burnett, *The Romantick Lady* (London: Charles Scribner's Sons, 1927), 316; hereafter cited in text.

2. *Sara Crewe; or, What Happened at Miss Minchin's and Editha's Burglar* (London: Frederick Warne, 1888), 27; hereafter cited in text as *Sara.*

3. *The Little Princess: A Play for Children and Grown-up Children in Three Acts* (1911; New York: Samuel French, 1939), 6; hereafter cited in text as *Play.*

4. Ann Thwaite, *Waiting for the Party: The Life of Frances Hodgson Burnett* (London: Secker & Warburg, 1974), 105; hereafter cited in text.

5. Phyllis Bixler, *Frances Hodgson Burnett* (Boston: Twayne Publishers, 1984), 89; hereafter cited in text.

6. *The One I Knew the Best of All* (1893; London: Frederick Warne, 1974), 100; hereafter cited in text as *Best.*

7. Martin Green, *Dreams of Adventure, Deeds of Empire* (New York: Basic Books, 1979), 3.

8. Edward Said, *Culture and Imperialism* (New York: Alfred A. Knopf, 1993), 53; hereafter cited in text.

9. Jacqueline Bratton, "British Imperialism and the Reproduction of Femininity in Girls' Fiction, 1900–1930," in *Imperialism and Juvenile Literature,* ed. Jeffrey Richards (Manchester: Manchester University Press, 1989), 197; hereafter cited in text.

10. Donald E. Hall, "'We and the World': Juliana Horatia Ewing and Victorian Colonialism for Children," *Children's Literature Association Quarterly* 16 (1991): 52; hereafter cited in text.

11. *A Little Princess* (Harmondsworth, England: Puffin, 1973), 8; hereafter cited in text.

12. Elizabeth Lennox Keyser, "'The Whole Story': Frances Hodgson Burnett's *A Little Princess,*" in *Triumphs of the Spirit in Children's Literature,*

ed. Francelia Butler and Richard Rotert (Hamden, Conn.: Library Professional Publications, 1986), 241; hereafter cited in text.

13. Mary Molesworth, *The Carved Lions* (1895; New York: E. P. Dutton, 1964), 8; hereafter cited in text.

14. Bruno Bettelheim, *The Uses of Enchantment: The Meaning and Importance of Fairy Tales* (New York: Alfred A. Knopf, 1976), 147; hereafter cited in text.

15. Augustine Birrell, "Notes about Books," *Atalanta* 1 (1887–88): 654.

16. *Bookman,* Christmas Supplement (1905): 34.

17. *Athenaeum,* 16 December 1905, 833.

18. *Spectator,* 16 December 1905, 1042.

19. Elaine Showalter, *A Literature of Their Own: British Women Novelists from Brontë to Lessing* (Princeton, N.J.: Princeton University Press, 1977), 338; hereafter cited in text.

20. Roger Lancelyn Green, *Tellers of Tales: British Authors of Children's Books from 1800 to 1964* (1964; New York: Franklin Watts, 1965), 120; hereafter cited in text.

21. Marghanita Laski, *Mrs. Ewing, Mrs. Molesworth and Mrs. Hodgson Burnett* (London: Arthur Barker, 1950), 85; hereafter cited in text.

22. Isabelle Jan, *On Children's Literature* (New York: Schocken Books, 1974), 102; hereafter cited in text.

23. Mary Cadogan and Patricia Craig, *You're a Brick, Angela! A New Look at Girls' Fiction from 1839 to 1975* (London: Victor Gollancz, 1976), 69; hereafter cited in text.

24. See Juliet Dusinberre, *Alice to the Lighthouse: Children's Books and Radical Experiments in Art* (London: Macmillan, 1987), 30–31 and 213–14.

25. Marian E. Brown, "Three Versions of *A Little Princess:* How the Story Developed," *Children's Literature in Education* 19 (1988): 199–210.

26. Phyllis Bixler, "Gardens, Houses, and Nurturant Power in *The Secret Garden,*" in *Romanticism and Children's Literature,* ed. James Holt McGavran, Jr. (Athens: University of Georgia Press, 1991), 217; hereafter cited in text.

27. Lynne Sharon Schwartz, Afterword to *A Little Princess* (New York: Signet, 1990), 233; hereafter cited in text.

28. Mavis Reimer, "Tales Out of School: L. T. Meade and the School Story." Ph.D. diss., University of Calgary, Calgary, 1993, 103; hereafter cited in text.

29. See Nancy Armstrong, *Desire and Domestic Fiction: A Political History of the Novel* (New York: Oxford University Press, 1987), 54.

30. *Racketty-Packetty House by Queen Crosspatch: Spelled by Frances Hodgson Burnett* (London: Frederick Warne, 1907), 1.

31. Bram Stoker, *Dracula* (1897; New York: Signet Classic, 1965), 182.

32. Mikhail Bakhtin, *Rabelais and His World*, trans. Helene Iswolsky (Bloomington: Indiana University Press, 1984), 70; hereafter cited in text.

33. Gerald Prince, *Dictionary of Narratology* (Lincoln and London: University of Nebraska Press, 1987), 9; hereafter cited in text.

34. U. C. Knoepflmacher, "Introduction," *Teaching Children's Literature: Issues, Pedagogy, Resources*, ed. Glenn Edward Sadler (New York: MLA, 1992), 1–2.

Bibliography

Primary Works

Works by Frances Hodgson Burnett

Barty Crusoe and His Man Saturday. New York: Moffat, Yard, 1909.

The Captain's Youngest, Piccino, and Other Child Stories. London: Frederick Warne, 1894.

Children I Have Known. London: James R. Osgood, McIlvaine & Co., 1892.

A Lady of Quality: Being a Most Curious, Hitherto Unknown History, as Related by Mr. Isaac Bickerstaff but Not Presented to the World of Fashion through the Pages of the Tattler and Now for the First Time Written Down. 1896. New York: Scribners, 1914.

The Land of the Blue Flower. New York: Moffat, Yard & Co., 1909.

A Little Princess: Being the Whole Story of Sara Crewe Now Told for the First Time. London: Frederick Warne; New York: Scribners, 1905. Reprinted, Harmondsworth, England: Puffin, 1973; New York: Signet, 1990.

The Little Princess: A Play for Children and Grown-up Children in Three Acts. 1911. New York: Samuel French, 1939.

The Lost Prince. 1915. Harmondsworth, England: Puffin, 1976.

The Making of a Marchioness. 1901. London: Anthony Blond, 1966.

Racketty-Packetty House by Queen Crosspatch: Spelled by Frances Hodgson Burnett. London: Frederick Warne, 1907.

Sara Crewe; or, What Happened at Miss Minchin's and Editha's Burglar. London: Frederick Warne, 1888. Reprinted, New York: Scholastic, 1963, 1974.

The Secret Garden. 1911. New York: Dell, 1973.

That Lass o' Lowrie's. 1877. New York: Scribners, 1888.

The Troubles of Queen Silver-Bell by Queen Crosspatch: Spelled by Frances Hodgson Burnett. London: Frederick Warne, 1907.

Works Influential to Burnett's Writing

Ballantyne, R. M. *The Coral Island.* 1857. New York: Oxford World's Classics, 1990.

Bowman, James F. *The Island Home; or, The Young Castaways.* 1851. Boston: Gould & Lincoln, 1852.

Brontë, Charlotte. *Emma.* An unfinished novel printed in *The Professor,* edited by Margaret Smith and Herbert Rosengarten, 303–25. Oxford: Clarendon Press, 1987.

———. *Villette.* 1853. Harmondsworth, England: Penguin, 1982.

Defoe, Daniel. *Robinson Crusoe.* 1719. New York: Harper & Row, 1965.

Dickens, Charles. *Bleak House.* 1853. New York: Signet Classic, 1964.

———. *A Christmas Carol.* 1843. New York: Bantam: 1983.

———. *Little Dorrit.* 1857. Toronto: Macmillan, 1969.

MacDonald, George. *At the Back of the North Wind.* 1872. New York: Airmont Classic, 1966.

———. *David Elginbrod.* London: Hurst & Blackett, 1871.

———. *Malcolm.* London: Cassell, 1927.

———. *The Lost Princess: A Double Story.* 1875. London: J. M. Dent, 1967.

———. *Phantastes.* 1858. London: J. M. Dent & Sons, 1983.

Marryat, Captain. *Masterman Ready.* 1841–42. New York: Garland, 1976.

Molesworth, Mary. *The Carved Lions.* 1895. New York: E. P. Dutton, 1964.

———. *Hermy: The Story of a Little Girl.* London: W. & R. Chambers, n.d.

Nesbit, E. *The Five Children and It.* 1902. Harmondsworth, England: Puffin, 1971.

———. *The Phoenix and the Carpet.* 1904. Harmondsworth, England: Puffin, 1971.

———. *The Story of the Amulet.* 1906. Harmondsworth, England: Puffin, 1980.

Reid, Mayne. *The Desert House; or, The English Family Robinson.* 1849. New York: E. P. Dutton, 1908.

Stoker, Bram. *Dracula.* 1897. New York: Signet Classic, 1965.

Wells, H. G. "The Door in the Wall." 1906. In *Selected Short Stories.* Harmondsworth, England: Puffin, 1971.

———. *The Sea Lady.* 1902. London: Methuen & Co., 1934.

Wyss, Johann David. *The Swiss Family Robinson.* Translated 1814. London: Partridge, n.d.

Secondary Works

Books

Bakhtin, Mikhail. *Rabelais and His World,* translated by Helene Iswolsky. Bloomington: Indiana University Press, 1984.

Barther, Roland. *S/Z.* Translated by Richard Miller. New York: Hill and Wang, 1974.

Bettelheim, Bruno. *The Uses of Enchantment: The Meaning and Importance of Fairy Tales.* New York: Alfred A. Knopf, 1976.

Bixler, Phyllis. *Frances Hodgson Burnett.* Boston: Twayne Publishers, 1984.

Burnett, Vivian. *The Romantic Lady.* London: Charles Scribner's Sons, 1927

Cadogan, Mary, and Patricia Craig. *You're a Brick, Angela! A New Look at Girls' Fiction from 1839 to 1975.* London: Victor Gollancz, 1976.

Dusinberre, Juliet. *Alice to the Lighthouse: Children's Books and Radical Experiments in Art.* London: Macmillan, 1987.

Frye, Northrop. *The Secular Scripture: A Study of the Structure of Romance.* Cambridge, Mass.: Harvard University Press, 1976.

Green, Martin. *Dreams of Adventure, Deeds of Empire.* New York: Basic Books, 1979.

Green, Roger Lancelyn. *Tellers of Tales: British Authors of Children's Books from 1800 to 1964.* 1964. New York: Franklin Watts, 1965.

Jackson, David. *Encounters with Books: Teaching Fiction 11–16.* London: Methuen, 1983.

Jan, Isabelle. *On Children's Literature.* New York: Schocken Books, 1974.

Laski, Marghanita. *Mrs. Ewing, Mrs. Molesworth and Mrs. Hodgson Burnett.* London: Arthur Barker, 1950.

Moore, Annie E. *Literature Old and New for Children.* Boston: Houghton Mifflin, 1934.

Prince, Gerald. *Dictionary of Narratology.* Lincoln and London: University of Nebraska Press, 1987.

Rowbotham, Judith. *Good Girls Make Good Wives: Guidance for Girls in Victorian Fiction.* Oxford: Basil Blackwell, 1989.

Sadler, Glenn Edward, ed. *Teaching Children's Literature: Issues, Pedagogy, Resources.* New York: MLA, 1992.

Said, Edward. *Culture and Imperialism.* New York: Alfred A. Knopf, 1993.

Showalter, Elaine. *A Literature of Their Own: British Women Novelists from Brontë to Lessing.* Princeton, N.J.: Princeton University Press, 1977.

Thwaite, Ann. *Waiting for the Party: The Life of Frances Hodgson Burnett.* London: Seckor & Warburg, 1974.

Trease, Geoffrey. *Tales Out of School: A Survey of Children's Fiction.* 1949. London: Heinemann, 1964.

Articles and Parts of Books

Birrell, Augustine. "Notes about Books." *Atalanta* 1 (1887–88): 653–54.

Bixler, Phyllis. "Tradition and the Individual Talent of Frances Hodgson Burnett: A Generic Analysis of *Little Lord Fauntleroy, A Little Princess,* and *The Secret Garden.*" *Children's Literature* 7 (1978): 191–207.

———. "Frances Hodgson Burnett." In *Dictionary of Literary Biography,* vol. 42, *American Writers for Children before 1900,* 97–117. Detroit: Gale Research, 1985.

———. "Gardens, Houses, and Nurturant Power in *The Secret Garden.*" In *Romanticism and Children's Literature,* edited by James Holt McGavran, Jr., 208–24. Athens: University of Georgia Press, 1991.

Bratton, Jacqueline. "British Imperialism and the Reproduction of Femininity in Girls' Fiction, 1900–1930." In *Imperialism and Juvenile Literature,* edited by Jeffrey Richards, 195–215. Manchester: Manchester University Press, 1989.

Brown, Marian E. "Three Versions of *A Little Princess:* How the Story Developed." *Children's Literature in Education* 19 (1988): 199–210.

Burnett, Vivian. *The Romantick Lady.* London: Charles Scribner's Sons, 1927.

Hall, Donald E. "'We and the World': Juliana Horatia Ewing and Victorian Colonialism for Children." *Children's Literature Association Quarterly* 16 (1991): 51–55.

Keyser, Elizabeth Lennox. "'The Whole Story': Frances Hodgson Burnett's *A Little Princess.*" In *Triumphs of the Spirit in Children's Literature,* edited by Francelia Butler and Richard Rotert, 230–43. Hamden, Conn.: Library Professional Publications, 1986.

Schwartz, Lynne Sharon. Afterword to *A Little Princess,* 223–36. New York: Signet Classics, 1990.

Thwaite, Ann. "Frances Hodgson Burnett," *Writers for Children,* edited by Jane M. Bingham, 103–9. New York: Scribners, 1988.

Dissertation

Reimer, Mavis. "Tales Out of School: L. T. Meade and the School Story." Ph.D. dissertation, University of Calgary, Calgary, 1993.

Reviews of *A Little Princess*

Athenaeum, 16 December 1905, 833.

Bookman, Christmas Supplement (1905): 34.

Spectator, 16 December 1905, 1042.

Index

Index

The Author

Roderick McGillis is a professor of English at the University of Calgary. He is the editor of *For the Childlike: George MacDonald's Fantasies for Children* (1992) and the author of *The Nimble Reader: Literary Theory and Children's Literature* (1995) and essays on various aspects and periods of children's literature. He has served as editor of the *Children's Literature Association Quarterly* and as president of the Children's Literature Association.